DO NOT REMOVE
CARDS FROM POCKET

I HAVE A PLACE

Life with a Younger Man
by Irma Wallem

Mercury House, Incorporated
San Francisco

Copyright © 1988 by Irma Wallem

Published in the United States by
Mercury House
San Francisco, California

Distributed to the trade by
Kampmann & Company, Inc.
New York, New York

Earlier versions of "Fear of Falling" and "How to Live with an Unmarried Man" appeared in ZYZZYVA (San Francisco, Spring 1987).

Mercury House and colophon are registered trademarks of Mercury House, Incorporated

Manufactured in the United States of America

Library of Congress Cataloging-in-Publication Data

Wallem, Irma, 1908–
  I have a place : life with a younger man / by Irma Wallem.
    p. cm.
  ISBN 0–916515–44–3 : $14.95
  1. Wallem, Irma, 1908–   . 2. Roommates—United States—Biography. 3. Aged women—United States—Biography. 4. Middle aged men—United States—Biography. 5. Interpersonal relations. I. Title.
HQ975.5.W35 1988
646.7–dc19   88-5376
                                                        CIP

Many people have taught me that you don't write books all by yourself. It takes loving friends to listen and encourage, a teacher like Howard Junker, now editor of ZYZZYVA, along with editors like the ones at Mercury House. My thanks to Alev, Zippie, Loralee, and the three Carols. Then there is Bernard, the world's only secretary who can neither type nor spell, but who has beaten a path to the post office.

Introduction

There has never been a day since Phillip came to share my home that he hasn't been free to roll up his sleeping bag and move on. I know that if I asked him to leave, he would quietly take off down the road to some new experience. This is because we do not have that *piece of paper*.

Phillip came into my life three years and eight months ago — a homeless, hungry, forlorn young man with uncut hair but beautiful manners, gentle ways, and an unusual past. My women friends and the people at church were surprised when I let him stay, but that day was an end of loneliness for both of us. From the very first, he seemed to belong. My dog Molly liked him, and she was a good judge of character.

Phillip and I are very different. In his forties, he is half my age, though at times I feel younger than he is. I like the closeness of a small town like ours; he once thought life was only worth living in a city. (My grandmother once told me I like being a big fish in a small puddle. Phillip's puddle is the world.) I am a person who loves home; Phillip has traveled and wandered and explored. I have had two husbands, two daughters, and three stepdaughters; Phillip has never been married. I am a morning person; he concentrates best at night. I like to write letters; he reaches for the telephone. He likes rye bread; I like whole wheat. He scatters; I pick up.

But we both know how it feels to be lonely. We both know how good it is to have someone to come home to.

I ask Phillip, "What is the opposite of loneliness?"

"What you and I have together," he answers.

1

"What is the opposite of love?"

"Boredom."

Little traditions hold us together — pizza on Sunday nights, popcorn if it rains, the *San Francisco Chronicle* with all the extra pages taken out and the Datebook Section on top so Phillip can decide which television programs to watch.

But most of all, we are held together by *talk*. Phillip walks the floor in the evening after we've turned off the television and tells me all the things that have happened to him. He has never told it all before. Once a priest urged him to go to confession. "If I did that, he would think I was bragging," Phillip says. But I know he is truthful, because who could make up the stories he tells?

And I tell him my stories, less daring and unusual than his, but with the same spirit of adventure my parents knew as part of the pioneer culture.

Our stories make up a kind of patchwork quilt, weaving our lives together. We try to make sense out of our mistakes, so that we won't make them again, and to remember and treasure the good times. We tell each other about experiences that shaped our thinking. We meet new people and puzzle ourselves about what makes them tick. We play word games.

"Name a turning point," I say.

He names V-Day in 1945, when he stood with his mother on a street in Algiers, watching the Victory parade. People were laughing and crying. Women held out gifts of sweet rolls and flowers and tried to catch the hands of soldiers. Now and then an American soldier would fall out of line for a hug. Planes flew close overhead, but now they were dropping fluttering masses of small Allied flags. Phillip broke loose from his mother and picked up a red, white, and blue one with stars in the corner. At that moment, he decided to come to America.

Until then, he had associated Americans with peanut butter. One week when the people in Algiers had no food at all, the Americans had smuggled in big vats of peanut butter and he had heaped a huge pile on his plate. That week, everyone was constipated.

Had I been standing on that street, with my two small daughters beside me, Phillip's mother might have referred to me as *one of those peasants.* She taught Phillip to love music, art, and literature. I've always painted canvasses for people's walls and written stories, but music was never a part of my life. Now I like even some of the classics.

Phillip taught me to enjoy music, just as I have tried to bring some order and understanding and patience into his life. But mostly we have given each other someone with whom to share our stories and our lives.

I was alone before Phillip came into my life, and I would be lonely if he left. Living with an unmarried man isn't always easy, but the time we have spent together has made the colors on my patchwork quilt so much brighter.

Fear of Falling

When I wrote to my cousin Rachel in Wichita that I was no longer living alone, but was living in the same house with an unmarried man the same age as my youngest daughter, she was so concerned that she called me at once—long distance—though she lives on a fixed income. She thought the shock of my husband's recent death had caused one of those small strokes that do not cripple, but leave a personality change.

"We don't live *together*," I told Rachel. "He lives *with* me."

"Well?"

"I believe God sent him," I hurried to explain. (Rachel is very religious.) I told her how Phillip had appeared on the very day that I stumbled and took a hard fall on the kitchen step, causing my knee to swell and giving me a limp.

Now, after three years, I write to Rachel every month. The women in her bridge club love to hear all about Phillip. One woman calls me a *free spirit*. They talk about the two of us while they deal out the cards.

As I said in one of my letters, I need *him* because of my fear of falling, and he needs *me* because of his fear of reaching—reaching for a cigarette or a glass of wine . . . and not finding it.

Somehow it was an even trade—from the very first.

* * *

For a few minutes after my fall I did not think I could get to my feet without help. I lay there, feeling the shock, hoping that when I did get up I would not feel that sharp jab of

4

pain that means a bone fracture. My dog, Molly, was beside me, licking my face and leaning her fat little brown body against me, as if she could help. At last I was able to pull myself up, limp into the kitchen, and wrap ice cubes in a towel to hold on my knee.

As I sat there on the kitchen stool, Molly gave a low growl. A dark, bearded man was looking at me through the screen door. I had forgotten to latch it, but I felt no fear. This man looked so forlorn and weary he could hardly be capable of rape or murder. He might even be starving, while I had food going stale. During the Great Depression, when we lived in Oklahoma, tramps often came to the back door and we always fed them. I couldn't let this man just stand there.

"Come in," I said. "You look as if you're about to faint."

He stepped inside the door without saying a word.

I pointed to the refrigerator. "Pour yourself a glass of milk. Take that clean glass on the drainboard." I pointed to my knee with the ice cubes bound into a towel. "I can't get up."

I watched as he drank the milk slowly, looking out the window, not meeting my eyes. His bedroll was still looped about his shoulders and his black hair hung loose below his ears.

He seemed about forty. His brown shirt and jeans were soiled and wrinkled. His hand trembled as he placed the empty glass on the drainboard. Then he faced me and lifted his shoulders a little as he thanked me. His face was still drawn.

"How far have you walked?" I asked.

"About ten miles today, I guess."

I sat there for a minute, remembering all the warnings my daughter Karen had given me about letting strangers into the house. But he looked so tired.

"You can go into the living room and rest on the couch," I said.

I saw the sudden look of relief on his face, but he said nothing as he passed me. I heard a soft thud and knew that he had removed his shoes.

My television was in the living room. It was time for afternoon soap operas. I put the wet towel and the nearly melted ice cubes in the sink and tiptoed to my easy chair. My visitor lay on the couch, his eyes closed. He was scarcely breathing. He *had* removed his shoes, and there was a hole at the big toe of one of his black socks.

I kept the sound low for two whole hours of my programs before he made a slight movement. I tiptoed into the kitchen to start supper. I was peeling potatoes at the sink when I looked up to see him blinking in the doorway, as if he wondered where in the world he might be.

"Do you like fried potatoes?" I asked.

He gave a low laugh. "I could eat any kind of potatoes three times a day."

"That is what Jess used to say," I told him. "He was my second husband." I suddenly remembered that I didn't even know his name. "I'm Irma Wallem."

He put out his hand. "Just call me Phillip, no one can ever remember my last name, or pronounce it."

"You're welcome to stay for supper." I pointed down the hall. "The bathroom is the second door."

Already it seemed natural for Phillip to be in my home. I set the kitchen table with two places. I opened a can of pork and beans to go with the fried potatoes and set out the cucumber pickles. Everything was ready when he returned. He had dampened his hair and pushed it behind his ears. His shirt was buttoned close at the neck so he looked neater.

"What do you drink with your meals?" I asked. "Shall I make some instant coffee?"

He stood with his hand on my chair, hesitating. "I prefer wine, if you have it."

I gave him a quick look, not sure if I had heard correctly.

He smiled at me as if his request were well within my power to satisfy.

I reached way to the back of the kitchen shelf and got out my red cooking wine. "This bottle may have a few dregs," I said. I got down two of my stemmed glasses and added an ice cube to one of them to weaken my drink.

"No ice for me," Phillip said. "Red wine should be room temperature."

During that first meal I did most of the talking. Phillip was busy eating, but he looked up often to encourage me. If Jess had been there, he would have turned me off. He'd have said, "You're talking when you ought to be listening."

I told Phillip how my husband and I had been caretakers of the surrounding estate and how when he died just three months before, they had let me stay on because I couldn't decide what I wanted to do. My daughter Karen thought I should move into the town of Sonoma and live in an apartment where someone could check on me every day to see if I'd fallen. She was always reading in the papers about some woman who fell in the bathtub and lay for days with a broken hip. My daughter Lenni, who lived in Portland, had offered me a home in her basement.

I explained to Phillip how staying here was costing me — I had to hire a college student every week to do the pruning and keep down the weeds. He charged $6 an hour.

Phillip explained to me that he was walking to the wine country, where he hoped to find a job setting out grape vines. "I have to get started before it gets too dark," he said, but he didn't make a move to leave the table.

I sat there thinking how his feet would stumble along the road in the dark, and how the headlights would glare into his eyes. "A speeding car could hit you," I said.

"There's a moon."

I waited a little while. "You might as well put your sleeping bag in the tool shed," I told him.

"If that's what you want."

The next morning I was up and working in the kitchen two hours before I saw Phillip close the shed door and head along the path to the road with his bedroll across his shoulders.

I called out to him, "Stop and have some breakfast."

He paused and hurried toward me, removing his bedroll and taking a paper sack from inside it. At the door he stopped. "How is your knee this morning?" he asked.

"Much better." The fact was, I'd almost forgotten I'd been hurt.

He held up his sack. "I have a razor. Do you mind if I use your bathroom again?"

I nodded. "I'll fix you some eggs for breakfast. How do you like them?"

"Over easy," he answered quickly. He walked briskly down the hall. When he returned, I'd cooked him two strips of bacon and had the eggs ready to fry. I gave Phillip a quick, sideways look and saw that he had shaved and had even trimmed his Vandyke beard. "I used your scissors," he said. "I hope you don't mind."

He stood behind my chair while I set his food on the table and poured myself a glass of orange juice. Then, just as if we'd been in a restaurant, he pulled my chair out for me and pushed it in carefully.

I watched him cut into the yolk of his egg. It was still runny. He looked up and smiled at me. "Not many women know how to cook an egg the way you do," he said.

I had cooked them that way for Jess the last twenty years, but he'd never bragged on me.

I noticed Phillip's eyes turned to my kitchen radio as he took the last bite of egg. "Would you like some music?" I asked.

He was on his feet at once, tuning until he found something soft. He poured me another cup of coffee, got out his pack of cigarettes, and offered me one. I saw he had only two left, but I took one and let him light it with his limp book of matches. I knew I wasn't likely to get the habit at my age.

We sat in silence, just listening together. At last Phillip stood up and pushed his chair back under the table. His eyes met mine. "Thank you for the breakfast and the good company," he said. "May I do something for you before I take off?"

I thought of all the lifting and carrying jobs I was saving for the college student when he came. But I shook my head. If Karen knew about him, she would say he had already worn out his welcome.

Molly got up from under the table, where she always stayed now that Jess was not there to make her get out. She followed Phillip to the door, wagging her tail as she waddled. She gave a low, yearning bark. Phillip reached down from adjusting the strap on his bedroll to pat her head.

"You can work in the rose garden a couple of hours," I said. "I might as well pay you as the college student."

Phillip let the bedroll fall to the ground. "I saw a rake and hoe in the shed. I'll go get them."

"You can give the rose bushes a last good watering," I said. "It should rain next month."

I watched from the window as he turned on the water and moved the hose about. He pulled the dry weeds with his bare hands, and I wished I'd thought to find him an old pair of Jess's gloves, but I'd given most of his things to Goodwill or burned them.

When I looked at the clock, the two hours were almost up, so I got my purse from my bedroom dresser drawer to pay Phillip when he came in.

Then I heard Molly's happy yip. Phillip stood in the doorway, holding a pink rose. "The very last perfect rose in the garden," he said. "I picked it for you."

I found a tall white vase. We sat there with the rose between us.

"There's a poem, 'The Last Rose of Summer.'"

"I know, 'Left blooming alone.'"

"When and where did you read a poem like that? It's from my generation."

"I read poetry in libraries. They're free, and they always have heat."

I closed my eyes, picturing Phillip in a library, maybe cold and hungry, his clothes wrinkled and his bedroll outside the door, reading poetry.

I looked down and saw that his tennis shoes were soaked. I got a section of the Sunday paper and spread it on the floor. "Take off your shoes," I ordered. "And your socks, too." The hole was still in that toe. "I'll see if I can find an old pair of Jess's socks, unless you have a pair in your bedroll."

He gave a short laugh. "I travel light," he said. "When a pair of socks get holes, I throw them away and get a new pair."

I went to find a rolled-up old pair of Jess's that I had planned to use for dust cloths. He put on the socks with the damp shoes over them, and we sat there with the rose between us.

I looked up at the kitchen clock and saw that it was time for lunch. I made bacon and tomato sandwiches, which we ate with the last of the cooking wine. As Phillip stood up to leave, he thanked me again, and I took twelve dollars from my purse, along with four quarters I had saved for the laundromat. Molly walked along the road a little way with him. When he reached the highway, he turned and waved. I waved back.

After Molly got back, the two of us went into the bedroom for our after-lunch naps. After a little while I got up and headed for the living room to watch my soap operas. When I looked toward the garden, I saw that water was running across the road! Phillip must have forgotten to turn off the hose. The rake lay flat on the ground with the teeth up. I hurried out to turn off the water and put the rake in the shed. My knee was starting to hurt again.

It was just as well, I thought, that this stranger had gone. He was not as reliable as the college student.

Then my soap operas were over, and the news came on. I limped into the kitchen and stood there looking into the refrigerator, trying to decide what I wanted for supper.

Molly gave her warning bark and ran to the door.

Phillip was there with a large paper bag in his arms. He came in and put the bag on the table, taking out a bottle of red wine, three packs of cigarettes, a *TV Guide,* and an oblong box. I took off the wrapping and found it was a box of Sampler chocolates. How could he have guessed they were a weakness of mine?

He sat there patting Molly while I rushed at supper. I took out the frozen fish sticks, opened a can of garden peas, and peeled two potatoes.

After supper we carried the wine and cigarettes and candy out to the garden. My white iron table and chairs had stood unused all summer. Phillip brushed off the dry leaves, and I went back to the kitchen to get our stemmed glasses and the ashtrays. Molly lay on the ground between us, and every now and then I put my hand down and touched her. We talked and somehow it was as if I had never really talked before.

At last I said, "You can stay on another night if you want. You might as well sleep in my husband's old room, I've put clean sheets on the bed."

* * *

It was another two weeks before it was warm enough to sit outside again. I sat at the iron table with my sweater over my shoulders. We were listening to a new Carly Simon tape. Phillip was in love with her voice and he shared her with me as we sat, hooked up with earphones to his new Walkman, the one he bought with the money I gave him to buy shoes.

At last I started to get to my feet. "I have to get back to reality," I said. "The supper dishes won't do themselves."

Phillip jerked to his feet. "But this *is* reality," he said. "We do work so we can enjoy *this*."

I sat down again and stayed until the chill drove us both inside. I did the dishes the next morning.

Memory of that night in the moonlight with Carly Simon is a kind of wonder to me. At this time in my life I hardly expected anything like that. The best I had hoped for was lack of arthritis and my daily soap operas.

How to Live with an Unmarried Man

I try to recall the minute when Phillip's presence began to take over my life. It may have been the morning at the sink when he came in and said, "I think I'm in need of a hug."

But our togetherness is in no way physical. When I try to define my feelings for Phillip, I am careful not to say I *love* him. I say, "I love him like a mother . . . a teacher . . . a part wife, an almost sweetheart." I want to unravel the feelings like strands in a rope.

One reason is that we are a most unlikely couple. Phillip is thin and dark, with intense brown eyes; I might be called a motherly type, with time showing on my face, near-gray hair, and years of vanilla ice cream showing on my figure. I once roamed the Ozark woods; he knows the streets of Paris. When he came to stay with me, he was forty-two and I was seventy-six.

On those first trips to town and to church, when my friends saw us together, I realized they didn't know whether to be amused or shocked.

Later, when they were used to seeing us together, and had a chance to talk with Phillip, they seemed relieved. They now had one less lonely widow to worry about.

I say to my friends, "He is the son I never had." But even as I say it, I know that in many ways I am younger than Phillip and he is older than I am. My life experiences are stretched out; his are squashed together.

I ask Phillip, "Do you think it is possible to feel both young and old at the same time?"

He looks at me with understanding. "When I was five

years old, I was impatient with my age. I knew I was old, but nobody else did."

We play the turning point game. We both have keen memories of small but important incidents that changed our outlooks. Somehow this filling-in gives us a sense of always having been together.

Until Phillip's sister and brothers were born, he was very protected and alone. He thought everybody liked him. Then one day when his cousins came to visit, there was an argument about one of his toy soldiers and his cousin hit him. He ran crying to his mother.

"How many times did he hit you?" she demanded.

"Twice," he answered.

"Did you hit him back?"

Phillip hung his head. "No."

His mother gave him two sharp slaps, which amazed him.

"For every time someone hits you and you don't hit back, I'll hit you double," she said.

It was a lesson he never forgot. Later, when he lived in Chicago, he took up featherweight boxing. He learned speed and gained strength in his arms. He learned to look punks in the eye and to hit first.

But he remembers another side to his mother, and how she taught him about the world around him. One day, as he fingered the silk of her dress, he asked, "How do worms make silk?"

She didn't answer at first, but the next day she brought him a small box filled with silkworms. For days he watched them at work. This instilled in him a respect for tiny creatures. When I once carelessly destroyed a spider's web on the back porch, he got angry with me.

I trade a turning point of my own. I was an only child and I was used to having my wishes granted. One day I heard my mother mention that we were having beans for supper. All afternoon I built up an expectation of good brown beans, cooked with sidemeat and lots of the brown juice that I loved to spread over my bread, like gravy.

As I took my place at the table I saw the bean bowl, but this time it contained green string-beans, the kind I hated.

The shock was too much for me. I pushed back my chair and rushed from the room. Upstairs, I pulled my small suitcase from the closet and packed my nightgown, my house slippers, my paper dolls, and my second-grade reader.

I was half a mile down the road before I knew it was hopeless, that I couldn't run away. I turned around and walked back. I sneaked in the back way, left my suitcase on the bed, and returned to the dining room, where Mama was clearing the table.

Without a word, she buttered me a slice of her home-made lightbread and sprinkled on sugar and a dash of cinnamon. I remember that day, because for at least thirty minutes I had had the wonderful feeling that anything was possible, that I really could run away.

* * *

That very first week, Phillip told me he had never been married, but that he had lived with a number of women. All of them had beautiful names—Charlene, Maria, Annabelle—or was it just the way he pronounced them, slowly, as if each name brought up a pleasant memory? They must have been lonely when he took off.

So I ask him, "Of all the women you've known, wasn't there one you wish you hadn't thrown back? Wasn't one so loving and kind you wish you'd married her and tried to make a go of it?"

"I've known many who were loving and kind. I probably won't ever talk about them, not even to you."

"So what you tell me is only the tip of the iceberg," I say. I won't press him, but one thing I know: He may exaggerate, but he doesn't lie.

Once he said to me, "You give me space. You listen to me. You don't show any of those small jealousies that a man can feel."

Perhaps those women with the beautiful names tried to own Phillip. I can picture the kind of jealousies they might have shown. I wasn't always so clever at hiding my feelings as I am now.

The first time I recall feeling that blinding jealous pain that cripples the senses was when I was five years old. My mother had gone to stay a few days with my aunt, who was ill. As I placed the knives and forks on the table for supper I was very proud that I was taking my mother's place as mistress of the house. But then my father said, "I sure wish Mama would come home." Why is it that seventy years later, I can still feel the hurt of those words?

I remember pulling my fingernails down across the cheek of a second-grade friend because she played with another girl, after she had been *my* best friend all summer.

I had been married to my first husband, Richard, only a short time when jealousy struck. I had finally learned to do the breakfast eggs over easy, without puncturing the yolks, with the whites cooked, but not tough, and the toast a golden brown, not black. One morning Richard told me to sleep in, he wouldn't need breakfast. Next morning, the same thing happened. After a while I began to feel rejected.

One morning I went downtown to the store where Richard worked as a bookkeeper. I bought the bread and potatoes I needed for supper in the grocery department, and then I went back to the office where Richard usually sat, wearing his green eyeshade and leaning over the big ledgers. He wasn't there. The grocery clerk pointed to the small café across the street. "He's gone for his usual breakfast break," he explained.

Across the street, I saw my husband being served by a smiling waitress in a white uniform. Her blond hair was held back in a net. She was wearing too much lipstick.

That evening when Richard came in through the back door I picked up one of my good wedding plates and threw it hard. It didn't break, so I threw the sugar bowl. It was days before I got all the sugar out of the dining room rug.

I think it is safe to say I will never throw a sugar bowl at Phillip, but that may be because I'm not married to him.

I think now, after more than three years of training, I could teach a college course on living with an unmarried man.

* * *

"I know I'm not easy to live with," Phillip says.

I don't answer that. I could make a list, starting with the way he spreads the newspaper all over the floor and doesn't pick it up when he is through reading. I guess if Jess had done that, I'd have complained. But with Phillip I pick up the paper and fold it again, neatly, hoping he'll take the hint, which he never does.

"I like being with you," he says. "You give me space."

I know so well what he means. I treasure the blocks of time he gives me. I am a morning person. I get up before sunrise and see the first pink of dawn. Molly and I walk down to the road and pick up the morning paper. I wait awhile until Molly finds a place where she has stopped before, and then we go in and I peel myself an orange, if it is the season for oranges.

Unless I want to watch a late night program with Phillip, I go to my room early and fall asleep at once. He stays awake and reads.

In the time we have together, we divide the tasks about the place. He peels the potatoes for the stew, which he says is the best he's ever eaten. He listens intently if I have time to give him cooking lessons. That is because someday he won't have me to cook for him.

I prefer to wash the dishes. He works too fast and I don't want any of my good dishes broken.

I've come around to having wine with my meals, but I always add an ice cube. He will eat brown beans now, but he never had them as a child.

My dog Molly doesn't really like anyone but me, but she permits Phillip to hold her as he watches television. He holds her close, as if she were a small child. "Have you ever had a child?" I ask him. We are sitting far apart in the room, giving each other space.

"I'm not sure," he says. "A few times I didn't stay around long enough to find out."

I am quiet then, aware that he knows what he has missed.

"What does it feel like to have a baby?" he asks.

"Awful," I say. "But I'm glad I went through it."

"It must have been terrible for my mother," he answers. "When I was first born they thought I was dead. They put me on a table and the doctor worked on my mother. Then a nurse saw my hand move and she spanked some life into me. They took us home that night and the next day the hospital was bombed to the ground."

We fall silent again and our eyes meet. I know that Phillip is thinking along with me that our coming together as we are could only have been planned by some higher power.

"The bombs just missed our house," Phillip adds. "My mother told me that all the other houses in the neighborhood were rubble."

I then tell Phillip about the *ifs* in my life that I thought at the time were mistakes. "But maybe our lives are all planned for us," I say. "It could be that it was planned so that we could be together at this special time in our lives."

Phillip nods. "I believe that," he says.

The Art Institute

Phillip had been with me only a few days when we discovered something we had in common. We had both attended the Art Institute of Chicago. I was there in the winter of 1934, and he in the fall of 1959. The thought that we had stared out the same windows, maybe sat in the same chair, became a strong bond between us.

My high school in Elk City, Oklahoma, didn't have any courses in art, but that hadn't stopped me from drawing pictures in study hall. I kept a pad of plain paper under my Ancient History book and took it out when the teacher wasn't watching. I made pencil drawings of all the students sitting around me. They knew what was going on, even if I fooled the teacher. When the bell rang and I went into the hall, everyone gathered around for peeks at the faces I'd drawn. There would be giggles and protests as some girl recognized her pug nose or her spit curl. Most of my faces turned out to resemble Colleen Moore or Gloria Swanson.

One day, early in my senior year, I came upon a group of oil paintings set on easels in the front hall. A lettered poster explained that the artist was Miss Bess Bradley, who would give private lessons in oil painting. The cost was one dollar a lesson.

Miss Bradley's pictures were of lakes and rivers and snowy mountains. I felt I could paint just as well as she did if only my parents would provide the money. I needn't have worried. My father went all out to buy the paints, brushes, and canvas on the list of supplies. He even went to the lumber yard and got samples of picture molding so he could make frames as soon as I supplied the pictures.

19

Miss Bradley had a box of studies. For my first painting on canvas I selected a snow scene with mountains and a lake with reflections of pine trees. It took three lessons to complete it. I carried it down the hall while it still smelled delightfully of turpentine. Two girls who stopped me to admire it decided then and there to take art, though they said they could never expect to do as well as I did. I didn't bother to tell them that, although I put in the background, Miss Bradley had added the finishing touches to my painting. She had taken my brush and worked on the tree branches and the reflections. I could keep a secret.

My parents got their money's worth. By the end of my senior year our house had at least one painting in every room. Grandma had one over her couch, and she bragged to everyone that her artist granddaughter had painted it "without a pattern." My aunts and uncles and two of my cousins also had samples of my work. Mama would look at each new painting as if to ask, "What has God wrought?"

I tried to be modest. I knew there were artists out there in the world who could do better than I could—Maxfield Parrish, for instance—but I could copy almost any picture unless it had a figure or a horse in it.

*   *   *

It was a long way from Oklahoma to the Art Institute of Chicago, but I made it . . . one cold January day, after two years in teachers' college and two years teaching in a rural school. I had felt that life was going past me and that if I was ever to be a great artist I would have to leave the Oklahoma dust storms and the sight of all the farmers setting off for California. I had saved $340, which seemed like more money than almost anyone had in 1934.

I couldn't take my oils with me as samples of my work, as directed, because they were all framed and hanging on my relatives' walls, so I made drawings and watercolors and carried them flat in the bottom of my suitcase. My work was supposed to prove to the registrar that I was ready for the advanced classes.

I arrived a week ahead of time and found myself a room within walking distance of the Art Institute. The room was three flights up. It had a small sink, a narrow bed, and one burner for light cooking. It was heated by steam, which rattled and hissed in the night. The bath was down the hall.

I used my week to try to get the feel of the city, riding on the bus to the end of the line, then paying return fare and going back. Each day was colder and grayer than the last, with colder and colder blasts off the Lake, but I was on a high, about to become a great artist.

On registration day, I walked up the broad concrete steps with the two guarding lions watching me and eventually found a man at a desk who calmly and with no expression on his bland face explained that I should first enter the lower school, not the advanced classes. He explained that I needed a *foundation*.

That first week I had the feeling I was returning to kindergarten. We did almost nothing but circles and squares. In drawing class we made circles and shaded them to show the third dimension, or filled little boxes with different shapes to learn composition. In watercolor class we did clear washes and then cut each color into small circles for a color wheel.

Life class was different. With my registration slip in hand, I found the right number on a closed door. I opened the door to see a completely naked woman standing at the front of the room with her arms up and her head back. I closed the door and fairly ran down the hall in a panic. It took ten minutes before I could collect myself and re-enter the room with dignity.

Almost all the students were, like me, from outside the city, and had to get that *foundation* that was so slow and deflating.

Miss Spencer, the drawing teacher, seemed to have given her life to *perspective* and *source* of light. We made endless circles and shaded them to show third dimension. Miss Spencer never walked about the room, as I had done the two years I taught second grade. She sat at her desk like a queen and made corrections as we lined up to show our pencil work. Nothing pleased her. When we left her room, we walked away with spirits cast down.

There were no mountains and lakes to paint in water-color class. We painted apples and cups and blue vases, nothing to hang on walls. Composition was made up of shaded masses, cut through with lines. No hills and trees, nothing resembling reality. It seemed like a kind of sin to draw a real tree with branches and leaves.

Life class was speed and action, stick figures with no faces. It didn't matter whether the model was beautiful; it was easier if she was fat or scrawny.

Making friends was a slow process. Some of the students were just out of high school, while I had teachers' college and two years of teaching behind me. I was alone in the city, with the excitement of my new adventure long gone.

I had always been told I had talent, but now I wasn't so sure. My third-grade teacher, Miss Durbin, had helped me decide to be an artist. She wore high-necked white lacy blouses and long, gored black skirts. She was very frugal with art supplies, and kept the tin boxes of watercolors too high on a shelf for us to reach, except on Friday afternoon. Then we were each given a cup of clean water and a sheet of white paper and the watercolors, along with a square of cloth for cleanup.

Miss Durbin asked us to look out the window and paint what we saw. It was spring, and there were green hills and clouds in the blue sky. First we were to dampen our paper and then make a blue wash. I followed directions, first using my brush to outline the shape of a cloud. I put in the distant hills and a low tree. I was studying my painting to decide what to put in next, when Miss Durbin came up behind me. She lifted my paper and took it to the front of the class.

"This is what I told you to do," she said. "See how nicely the mountains blend into the sky. See the nice cloud."

That afternoon I stayed to dust erasers while Miss Durbin mounted our pictures on black paper. She put mine right in the center of the bulletin board.

After that I went on to designing paper doll dresses in watercolor at home. I was best at that of all my friends.

I believed in myself.

In Chicago, I began to have doubts.

I was enrolled for the winter term, but before it was half over I had counted up my money, wondering if I would need to write home to my parents for more. I began to feel as deflated as a child's empty balloon. Art was a lover who had let me down. With rules to follow, all the magic was gone.

The Great Depression was all around me. I could hardly walk along any street without having a man in a droopy overcoat hold out his hand for a dime. I rode past the public library one night and saw an unforgettable sight — all the chairs were occupied by grown men, sitting upright, but not reading. They were asleep.

I read a newspaper ad for art classes at Hull House. They were free, so I enrolled there even though it meant riding miles on a bus and getting off in a gray, frightening part of the city. But it made me feel more like a real artist than I did in my classes in the Lower School. I went every Thursday night. In an upstairs room, about two dozen men and women worked silently in charcoal to get the likeness of a seated model.

Brian Barnes, much older and a much better artist than me, worked near me. I would stop my own work to observe how he touched the tip of a nose or shaded a mouth. At the close of class each night, a collection of quarters was taken up for the model, usually some old man who had been taken off the street. Brian always put a dollar bill into the hat.

As I started to leave for home one night, Brian came up behind me and offered to walk me to the bus. "It's pretty dangerous this time of night," he said.

We walked together. He carried his roll of charcoal paper under one arm, and guided my steps with his free hand. His strength and his bigness reminded me of my father. In just that minute, with Brian's touch reminding me of my father, I fell in love.

Now Chicago took on magic again. Though Brian had no car, we felt no need of one. It was enough just to take the bus on Saturday afternoons, to visit the Field Museum together, to go to art shows, to walk through Marshall Fields. When the weather grew warm, we sat in the park while Brian sketched the people passing by.

Brian had a job — making drawings for a catalog put out by a manufacturing company. And he did the most beautiful watercolors I had ever seen. He never tried to sell the paintings he did when he was with me: he gave them to me. I pinned them on my wall with thumbtacks and planned to keep them forever.

I did not enroll for the spring session at the Art Institute. I sent home for money to pay for my room and continued taking my portrait class at Hull House.

One Saturday afternoon Brian and I and two other couples went on a sketching trip to the sand dunes in Indiana. The others were a little in awe of Brian because he was a commercial artist, making money with his art. I loved that drive through small towns and past farms. It had been so long since I had been outside Chicago that I had almost forgotten how cows and horses looked.

At last we stopped at a place with a good view of the lake. Sailboats drifted beyond the grassy sand hills, and we hurried to take out our sketch books. Brian promised to do a watercolor of the sketches he was making so I would have something to remember of this beautiful, sunny spring day. Hunger finally drove us back to the car, where we built a small fire and roasted weenies. We finished off our feast with marshmallows, brown on the outside and soft and sweet and white on the inside.

"I want to get in one good sketch before the sun goes down," Brian said.

I followed and we found a ravine, away from the others but with a view of a ferry along the horizon. When his sketch was finished, we sat and watched the light fade. We could hear guitar music from a group farther down the shore. After a long silence Brian got up and excused himself to go behind a clump of bushes. When he returned, I went to find my own clump. I could see the other two couples sitting by the last of our fire. The silence was too good to break. Brian got up and stood against the darkness. I could see the outline of his broad shoulders and the tallness of him. He came to where I sat in the sand, and I know he felt how I was trembling.

"I have to tell you," he said, his voice very low. "I'm married. My wife and our six-year-old son have been away visiting with her mother in Texas."

The hurt went all through me. I knew now why he had waited all these weeks without kissing me. It no longer seemed to matter.

At last we stumbled through the sand to join the others. We sat very close in the back seat going home, four of us in the back, but I was hardly aware of anyone but Brian. It was daylight when we got to my place. "I'll see you tonight," Brian said.

I was able to sleep most of the day away. In the late afternoon, I heard a knock at my door. My heart beat in wild anticipation. I opened the door and saw a face so angry that my welcoming smile left my face. A woman stood there looking past me at Brian's watercolors on the wall. She was tall and thin and her hair was in a knot. She wore a dark flowered dress. She walked to the wall and pulled down each picture in turn, letting the thumbtacks roll across the floor. I knew then that Brian must have told her about me, and that she had somehow forced him to give her my address.

Without saying a word, she slapped me hard across the face.

Next day, I went back to Oklahoma. I had to get on the train and sit there on the velvet seats, with the foot rest and the sound of wheels taking me away from Brian. I had to look out the window as the towns and farms flashed by, knowing I would never see him again.

Painting to Please Others

"It was not the Chicago Art Institute and those *foundation* courses I lived through that made an artist out of me," I told Phillip. "It was my second husband, Jess . . . and an accident, caused by a pebble."

It took twenty-eight years of teaching school, of being a mother for my two girls and seeing them and my three stepdaughters married off, before I returned to my dream of painting pictures for people's walls.

The girls were scattered, with homes of their own, and my Mama had come to live with us in Sonoma.

It was early spring, and I was running a little late for school that morning. I reached into my closet and selected a dress I hadn't worn all winter, a dress with pink flowers on a blue background. It was a bit tight and narrow, but I didn't take time to change. When it was time for the children's recess and my coffee break, I hurried toward the teachers' room across the yard. Halfway there I lost my balance, slid, and went down hard. When I tried to get up the pain struck and I went down again.

It took only a few minutes for the ambulance to come and take me to the hospital. Two weeks later I went home on crutches, knowing that my teaching career was over, since I was near retirement age.

Mama did the cooking and dishwashing; Jess did the laundry and housecleaning. I was free to use my time to be creative, but I did not go back to trying to write stories as I had at other times when I was not teaching.

A few months before my accident Jess had rented a small art gallery across the street from the Sonoma Mission. He

invited local artists to display their paintings. He would try
to sell them and keep his commission of twenty percent.
Though I was teaching I had joined a local art group and
often sold a few paintings at the outdoor shows in the Plaza.
Jess had only six of my paintings to start off with. He was
no artist, but he needed something to do that would excite
him. He got a kind of creative satisfaction from each painting he framed and hung on a display wall. Most of all he
liked to make sales.

He soon learned that if he sold one of my paintings he
got to keep *all* the money, to other artists he had to hand
out most of it.

The day after I returned from the hospital with my
broken hip, I went on crutches to the garage where
unfinished oil paintings waited. I painted flat, on a big
table, with my wheelchair making me just the right height.
Jess brought our old black-and-white television set and
connected it where I could glance up now and then to see
the actors in my soap operas. He bought me a dozen new
white canvas boards and encouraged me. He bought
frames and set them around the room for me to fill.

At first I was at a loss to know *what* to paint. I could no
longer go out to the hills or set up my easel in front of
historic buildings. But I had photographs I had saved for
years—mountains and snow scenes from Colorado, desert
scenes from our trips. I used art books and searched
through magazines for ideas. My garage became an assembly plant, with twenty paintings at a time arranged against
the wall, waiting to be finished.

Jess listened to the comments from tourists who visited
his gallery. He learned that women wanted long horizontal
paintings to go over divans and up-and-down ones to hang
in hallways. They wanted small ones of animals and clowns
and Raggedy Anns to go in children's rooms. The men
wanted redwoods and seascapes and desert scenes. He saw
how some were drawn to daisy paintings and others could
not resist one of the brown owls I loved to paint.

In a few months my work replaced the paintings of the other artists. My prices were low, but volume made up the difference. We put the money back into supplies and frames.

The idea for *Home Shows* came when Jess and I gave his daughter Dolores three paintings for her new home in Sacramento. The neighbors said if I would bring more they might buy them — they did. One neighbor asked us to have a showing at her home. The idea spread to his older daughter, Sandra, who lived in Clovis. When I visited Karen in Reedley, I took along paintings to sell to her neighbors. Friends in Kingsburg and Merced bought more.

Jess had his own method of judging my landscapes. "If I look at a picture and I want to *go* there, I can sell it," he said.

Jess learned that if he showed my work alone, it had no competition. No one described me as a great artist; it was simply that my work filled empty places in bedrooms, over divans, and even in bathrooms.

I never knew what request a day might bring. A woman brought a photograph of a dog who had died. I painted it life size and she cried when she came to get it. A man brought a picture of the barn he had played in when a child, but which had burned. I painted a cross-eyed black cat for a woman to give as a gift to her sister as a joke. I did a picture of five pigs in a row for a mother to put over the table so she could remind her children not to eat like pigs.

People ordered pictures of Fisherman's Wharf and the Golden Gate Bridge and the Sonoma Mission. My biggest order of all was for 500 small oil paintings of owls for an owl tournament at the golf course. A picture was to go beside each plate.

For an anniversary present, I was asked to paint a cartoon of a couple in bed, their four sons in bed with them, and their daughter in a cradle beside the bed. I was told it was the hit of the party.

My heavy production became a kind of joke, with our sons-in-law saying Jess must beat me to make me turn out pictures so fast. Somebody compared me to Henry Ford. Sooner or later, everything I did sold. Often I was invited to walk through a house and see how my paintings fit, how they filled the empty places and matched the curtains. At times my work decorated an entire home, from hallway to bathroom, so that as I walked through the house I felt the pull of my own creations, remembering how each picture had grown from the blank paper or canvas, to the background, then shapes and final touches.

I never did well in competition with other artists. No movie stars bought my work and no collectors paid outlandish prices, but one young mother told me that she had bought a painting of mine, all blues and lavender trees along a river, before they bought their divan, because my painting was cheaper. And her little girl learned to say her first words as she traced her fingers over my landscape.

Jess's younger daughter, Nora, thought that now I was ready for a truly big show. It was to be in Alameda, with twenty percent of the proceeds going to the Junior League. The setting was to be around a pool, at a beautiful country club. For months I painted with this show in mind. I was filled with as much fear as if my primary students were about to put on a Christmas pageant at the Golden Gate Theatre. This was me, a little girl from Oklahoma, showing my work to men and women who had never heard of me, who must have gone to art galleries and museums and seen the paintings of real artists.

Jess and my son-in-law and some other young men unloaded my canvases and placed them on easels all around the pool. They set up a table for wine glasses and bottles. Jess set up a card table nearby to collect checks and stamp the Mastercards.

At five o'clock the guests began to arrive. They stood around in small groups, wine glasses in hand. Some looked at my pictures, others talked.

I could see the reflection of my bowls of flowers, my Golden Gate Bridge, my Sonoma landscapes in the pool. Some of my colors matched the pale red in the sky. Jess sat at his table with his order book open and his pencil in hand. Scenes of low points in my past flashed before my eyes, the way the events of a lifetime are supposed to pass before the eyes of a dying person. How terrible it would be if we had to load all my paintings back into the station wagon and the car and drive home through the traffic, no money even to pay for the frames.

I found the bathroom and hid there for a long time, not even brave enough to pray.

Nora finally found me there. She said she had been looking for me everywhere. "A woman wants a floral like the one in gold tones, but she wants you to paint it in blues," she said.

So at least one person was interested. I took a deep breath and went out into the night. I made out the form of an empty easel, then another. I blinked against the lights. The easels stood in a sad row. My show is over, I thought. All my paintings have been loaded back into our cars.

Then I saw Jess, bent over, writing in his book. Behind him was a line of people, all standing, holding paintings, waiting to pay. I had never seen Jess look so happy, or write so fast, as he took their checks and wrote out receipts. No matter what anyone ever said about me being just a hack who painted only to please others and not myself, I would never care. Jess had made an artist out of me.

Now it is Phillip who frames my paintings and stands back and comments on how the frames improve them. He does not like many of my paintings. After all, he has been in scores of galleries all over the country and has even been in the Louvre. But every once in a while he takes a liking to one I haven't yet finished. He stops me before I ruin it.

"Not bad," he says. "You should put a big price on this one. Ask at least $200 for it, or keep it."

There's no use trying to explain that if I did catch some magic in my painting I want it to go over someone's divan, someone who may not be able to afford a divan yet. To Phillip, Art was only a mistress who lured him on and then left him, lonely and insecure.

To me, Art is butter and eggs, a dream, and an itch that I had to scratch before I died.

Art as a Mistress

Phillip never went to high school. For a time he attended military school, but otherwise he was tutored at home. When the situation in Algeria became dangerous, his family moved to Paris. They left their land and home behind, and were forced to sell many of their possessions.

Phillip had been expected to go into the military like his father, his grandfather, and even his great grandfather; but his mother believed that he had artistic talent and brought him to Chicago, where she knew some influential people. She was able to pull strings and get him enrolled in the Art Institute. He was not even twenty years old and he knew very little English.

He found his art courses in the lower school just as uninteresting as I had almost thirty years earlier. But he was fascinated by the place. He spent hours studying the French Impressionists, learning how they made paint give out light and energy.

He yearned to work on bigger canvases and to experiment more than the Art Institute courses allowed, so he set up a studio in his rented room. He stretched yards of canvas on big frames that he made himself. The pictures were so large that they didn't fit on his table, so he worked on the floor. In his excitement, he often spilled paint on the linoleum. One day the landlady came up, saw the condition of her floor, and threatened to throw him out . . . until she noticed an abstract canvas of golden brown and black, with touches of yellow light.

"My favorite colors," she said. "That wouldn't look bad in my downstairs hallway, even if the picture doesn't make

33

sense. I guess I could exchange it for the damage you've done to my floor."

Phillip put a wire on the back and carried it downstairs. He hung it opposite the entrance, where it blended with the stairway rug and hall curtains.

After that first success, Phillip began to feel encouraged. He often became so engrossed in his work that he forgot to attend classes.

One Sunday he saw in the paper that there was to be an open-air art show on Jackson Street. He carried three of his unframed pictures through the streets, stopping often to shift the load. When he reached the show, he stood them against a wall. In his heart he knew his paintings were good—and he did not really want to part with them. He priced them each at $600. Then he walked away to see the rest of the show.

When he returned an hour later, a woman in a mannish brown suit and a straight-brimmed hat was standing beside his paintings.

"I want this one," she said, pointing to Phillip's favorite. It resembled a forest in tones of deep green and brown, but with none of the trees defined. In the distance was a small figure of a little girl with light all around her.

"How shall I make out the check?" she asked.

Phillip was so confused he couldn't remember his English, so he told her in French.

That made the woman look at Phillip with even more interest. "I'm sorry," she said. "I know a little French, but I need a few lessons. I'm planning a trip to Paris in the spring."

He took her check and read the signature: "Magdaline Harper."

She smiled at the way he pronounced her name. She handed him a business card with her home address; he saw that she was a psychologist.

The next morning, Phillip felt strangely restless. He didn't want to go to his class in composition; he was bored with making little sketches in little squares to show the teacher. He loved his own big canvases, but that day he did not even feel like mixing paint. Besides, he was out of several colors. He remembered his $600 check and felt rich. His mother had left him only enough money to get by on, and he had planned to call her soon and ask for more. Now he could spend his own money in any way he pleased. From the bank, he went into Marshall Fields and bought a black silk shirt and a pair of expensive shoes. He threw out his old shirt and sandals, then he hailed a cab and headed for Magdaline's address in Lake Forest.

Her face broke into a smile as she welcomed him. Now he saw that she was in her late thirties. Her hair was pale blond and she wore no makeup. Her eyes were brown and very intense. "I'm so glad you came," she said. "I had no idea how to find you. I have a buyer for another one of your paintings!"

She stood aside and pointed to the back of her large living room. "I hung your painting as soon as I got home last night. I'm going to have it framed. I had guests here last night for dinner and they were simply fascinated. I could have sold it. I told them it was painted by a famous young French artist. You are famous, aren't you? If not, you soon will be."

Phillip modestly denied being famous. Later, he allowed himself to be persuaded to stay for what Magdaline described as "leftovers." He was used to making do with canned soup or rice cooked in his room, so he ate and drank a little more than usual.

Magdaline kept refilling his wine glass. He learned that she was divorced, that her only son was away at boarding school, that she was alone except for a cleaning woman who came in twice a week.

She loved the way he pronounced her name. She loved it when he forgot and spoke in French. "How much do you charge for French lessons?" she asked. "I know a friend who pays six dollars an hour."

Phillip looked at his watch and they both laughed. She moved closer to him on the couch and fingered the silk of his new shirt.

"You bought this for me," he said. "I cashed your check."

"I'd like to buy you another," she said. "I love shopping for men."

He was so young and inexperienced that he failed to recognize the way she faced him, her mouth trembling, as a sign of desire. For an instant he felt himself stiffen, then he met her lips and a little later they moved into her bedroom. He had never before been in a bed with white satin sheets.

In the weeks that followed Phillip learned how it felt to be completely taken over by another person. Each time he went out of his room he was careful to dress the way Magdaline liked him to look. But he wore his old paint-spattered clothes when he painted far into the night. He was now producing paintings that sold. He met all the right people, and as he learned to speak more fluent English, he developed the sense of humor and the infectious laugh that I so love about him. He learned how it felt to have people gather about him, listening to his every word.

The only art class he remembered to attend was life class. He could see some sense in sketching live models.

Not needing money, he neglected to write his mother in Paris. When she got a notice from the Art Institute that he had failed all his classes except life, she made an angry telephone call. He tried to explain his great success, that he was selling paintings as fast as he could turn them out, but all his mother could understand was his failure.

Not long after talking to his mother, Phillip began to lose touch with his art. He found he could no longer copy himself from the memory of his other works. Nothing happened. His canvases came out dull and unsatisfying. He smeared over them and tried repainting. He got new canvases and stacked the rejects against the wall. He stopped taking orders and attending art showings. He slept a lot. He avoided Magdaline.

One morning he took out his money from where he had hidden it under the mattress, packed his suitcase, and left — for New Orleans, partly because that was the next bus out, and partly because he had heard that many people there spoke French.

At first, with plenty of money, his family name, and his ability to speak French, Phillip lived well. There were court-yard gardens, wrought-iron balconies, and soft-spoken women. When he became bored with social life, he bought art history books.

He put off counting his money for several months. Then he realized that he needed to make a step downward in his expenses. He sold his books and started relying on public libraries. He also discovered Bourbon Street, where, as he says, "there are more prostitutes than anywhere on earth."

His new project was to find out what made them tick. He found he liked them better than some of the society women he had known. Prostitutes did not try to flirt and they didn't try to own him.

He first met Simone as she stood on a street corner waiting for a cab. She had long black hair, done in a loose knot, and the wind was blowing strands about her face. She was as short as he was, and plump. Her dress was black, but it was simple, even elegant. He made a remark about the wind. She didn't answer, but she looked at him in a friendly way. He tried again, this time in French. Her eyes lit up. Before he knew it, they had discovered that their stories were almost the same. She too had come to America expecting more than she had found. He told her. "If I'd been a woman, I might be standing on this corner with you."

He saw a man coming toward them who he thought might be her manager, so he told her his address and hurried away.

Phillip now lived in a small room and did his own cooking, such as it was. The next day Simone brought him cheese and bread and wine, and they sat for hours, talking but not once touching. She came to visit him often, and it was always the same. She left the rest of the food and a five dollar bill on his little table. She helped him survive for several weeks.

Then he found a note from his landlady under his door, and he counted his money. If he paid now, he would have nothing left to rent a cheaper place.

He left early the next morning and found himself an empty shack in West Wego. He just took it over. As he sat on the one chair wondering what to do next, he saw a man drive up and stop in front of the shack. He was so well dressed that Phillip assumed he had come to collect the rent. But it proved to be someone else looking for a free place to stay.

John Gore had a car and a few cooking utensils. They set up housekeeping together. That lasted a while, until Phillip was down to the change in his pocket. Then he rolled up his pillow in his blanket with his clothes and a sack containing his razor and comb and set off one morning on foot.

That night, he slept in a cemetery overlooking a small town. It was the first night he had ever slept in a cemetery, but it was not the last. He found them good places to meditate, and his hunger often helped him to see visions.

At last hunger drove him down the hill into town. He found the one restaurant on the main street, went around back, and opened the lid of the garbage can. He found a half-eaten hamburger and devoured it.

"I had seen dogs tip over garbage cans," Phillip told me, "but I never thought I'd act that much like a dog. The can tipped over and I looked around, but nobody saw me. I ran back up the hill to the cemetery. It seemed like home."

The next morning he got up early and started walking to the next town. This time when he looked for food in the garbage can, the police arrested him for vagrancy. Though he had no money, he still carried his wallet with his mother's Paris address and phone number. The police called her, and she sent money for him to return home. He took the money, but he set off in the opposite direction with his bedroll on his back.

One-Suitcase Man

The first time Phillip asked for a button to sew on the cuff of his black shirt, I went into my bedroom and brought out my button box. It is the size of a shoebox, decorated with designs cut from wallpaper samples. He ran his fingers through the many-colored, odd-shaped buttons and found the exact size and color he wanted.

"I've never lived in a house with a button box," he said. "Where did you buy them all?"

"You don't go out and buy buttons to fill a button box," I explained. "The box was given to me by my mother-in-law for a wedding present. She decorated it and gave me half her supply of buttons. When Mama died I inherited a box of buttons from her, and I dumped them all in here together."

"I never saved a button in my life," Phillip said. "I don't even know what happened to all my old clothes."

"In the old days," I said, "we didn't give our clothes to the Salvation Army or Goodwill. We gave them to relatives or we wore them until they were threadbare. Then we cut off the buttons and saved them. And we ripped everything apart at the seams and cut up the good sections for quilt pieces. The worn parts we cut in squares and put in the rag drawer to use for dusting rags or dishcloths. You didn't go buy paper towels and Kleenex, and Sears Roebuck supplied the toilet tissue."

"I once had a leather jacket I designed myself," Phillip said. "I wish I knew what happened to it."

"You discarded it the way you did your girlfriends," I said.

I could see that that had hit home. "I planned to wear that leather jacket forever, but I probably left it the same place I left my good boots. I left in such a hurry I took only one suitcase."

The idea of discarding all my belongings except for one suitcase struck me with such a jumble of emotions I almost failed to pick up that Phillip was about to tell me some of his adventures.

                    *   *   *

For quite a few months of his life, Phillip lived in airports.

It all began one afternoon when he was alone in the small kitchen-bedroom and bath he shared with a girlfriend named Lana. She had left that morning, a little angry. As she took off in her starched green uniform to work her six-hour shift, he had still not picked up his socks, cleaned the kitchen, or made the bed. He knew she had a right to be angry, but he was suddenly tired of it all.

He was between jobs. That was one of the reasons he had slept late; he dreaded going out to look for work. He did have about $300 left on his side of the mattress, enough to buy himself a ticket to somewhere, if he could decide where he wanted to go.

He went to the airport and sat for a long time alone on a bench with his suitcase beside him. He thought of Lana and knew he was giving up a good thing. He was almost ready to catch the next bus back to the city when a man came and sat beside him. Phillip saw the man's suitcase before he got a good look at his face. The suitcase was plastered with labels from different countries. One read Paris. He turned to the man. "My mother lives in Paris," he said.

"Paris was my favorite city," the man said. For a time the two exchanged favorite streets and restaurants, but not names. Only when they discovered that both their fathers were colonels did they shake hands and introduce them-

selves. The man's name was Andrew Stevens. He was an
only son, and his family expected him to enter military
service in France very soon. Phillip explained that he had
also been sent to military school to become an officer, but
instead had come to America.

Andrew said that he was meeting his father in San Francisco in a few months to plan his future, but until then he
was going to see all he could of the United States.

Though he had been about ready to go back and face life
with Lana again, Phillip looked closely at Andrew and
decided he liked him better. Andrew was blond, with
freckles going up into his hair. He had a good face, open
and kindly. Even sitting down, Phillip could see that
Andrew was a head taller than he was. "I was born in
another country," Phillip said, "but I probably know more
about the United States than most Americans. I'd like to be
your guide."

"You mean you're completely free to travel?" Andrew
asked.

"I'm free."

Andrew explained that because of his father's job, he
could fly for free. Now he offered to pay Phillip's travel
expenses if Phillip would be his guide. The two shook
hands. They went to the bar and had a drink. Phillip
watched for any signs that Andrew might be an alcoholic.
He had learned to be wary of both men and women who
could not stop at one drink. They had only one. In the
cafeteria, they both chose meat and potatoes, good people-
food, not food fit only for rabbits. As they walked together,
past the shops, Phillip observed that Andrew wasn't "gay."
He looked at girls and they looked back with pleasure.

When they returned to pick up their suitcases, Andrew
asked, "Where are we going first?"

"How about O'Hare, in Chicago?" Phillip suggested.

"Sounds good to me," Andrew said.

O'Hare was just as Phillip remembered it, exciting and
full of interesting people. But he was also excited about

seeing Chicago as a tourist. It held many sweet and painful memories. They took a tour bus past the Art Institute, past the elegant homes on the North Shore. After a full day of being tourists, they slept on airport chairs. In the morning they used the rest room to shave.

The second day they toured past Hull House and the stockyards. By evening they were so tired that Andrew rented a hotel room and they slept through the third day. They spent the fourth day in the airport, just watching people come and go, entertaining each other by making up stories about the people they saw. Phillip remembers one woman well. She seemed to be saying farewell to her husband and small child, but then she went around a corner and met another man, whom she kissed and kissed.

Though Phillip could have made O'Hare his permanent home, Andrew wanted to see more.

"How about Disneyland?" Though Phillip had lived in California for years, he had never seen Disneyland.

"I thought that was for kids," Andrew protested, but they were soon on a night flight to Orange County. Andrew rented a room at the Disneyland Hotel. As they waited in the lines, Phillip would often lose patience and wander away. This didn't bother Andrew, who often wound up in the hotel room with a girl.

A week at Disneyland was all Phillip could take. He began to dream of Denver, cool even in summer. As their plane neared the Mile High City, Phillip tried to make out the place in the mountains where he had been snowbound with a woman named Sandra, but they were too high and too far away.

Their next stop was Salt Lake City, where they saw the Mormon world. Then New Orleans, with more bittersweet memories for Phillip.

"Airports are the cathedrals of the Space Age," says Phillip. "Each has its own personality, its own style."

"What about Las Vegas?" I asked.

"That airport," he said, "is like a beautiful whore who doesn't just take a man's money, but wants him to leave with his pockets empty." He and Andrew had sat there for hours reading faces. They saw people arriving in a state of great excitement, and others leaving with closed faces and looks of desperation.

They took in the shows, had their share of free drinks, and ate the best and cheapest food they had known on the entire trip. This was the one place in America where Andrew's good looks were hardly noticed. It gave Phillip some satisfaction to see him ignored in favor of the slot machines.

After three days in a hotel they returned to the airport and tried to decide what could follow Las Vegas. They bought a map and spread it on the floor. Phillip threw a coin that landed in the middle of Texas. So they flew to Dallas.

After one day of driving around, they returned to the airport. Andrew called his father, and got orders to report to San Francisco. Phillip had nowhere to go, and Dallas was not his idea of a place to find a job. He counted his money and settled for a bus ticket going north.

"On a bus you lose all the joy of travel," he told me. "There's no excitement in people's faces. They all know where they're going and there's no nonsense. They all look tired and married."

The bus took him into Oklahoma and then to the edge of Kansas. He rented a pillow for the night and staggered out at bus stops for coffee.

The bus stopped somewhere in Kansas at a town near a small airport. Small private planes were spread all about. With his suitcase in hand, Phillip walked across the edge of a wheat field and entered the waiting room. Three people sat reading magazines. He went into the empty rest room and shaved and changed his shirt, then walked back into the almost empty waiting room and set his suitcase down before he went into the bar.

Four or five men watched him as he ordered a drink. As he tasted it he said, "One thing I've learned about airport bars, they have the best bartenders in the world." Then he went on to mention drinks he had enjoyed at New York and Denver and even Paris. He used all his tricks to get conversation going.

After a while one of the pilots got up to leave. "I'm heading for Houston in a few minutes," he said. "If you want a ride, I'd be glad of some good company."

Phillip waited for what he described as a decent length of time before he answered. "I might be able to make connections in Houston."

Phillip calls the next few weeks the second phase of his one-suitcase airport existence. He learned that pilots of private planes are often lonely and therefore more than glad to give a free ride to someone, provided they are good company. Now and then, he got into a game of cards and won enough money to rent a hotel room, sleep for hours, and enjoy a shower. He would wash his shirt and let it dry while he slept. He usually threw away his socks and bought new ones. If he spent a night in an airport, he would walk into town in the early evening and try to find a library that stayed open late. Sometimes he took in a movie. The evening was his lonely time. He would walk by houses where the dining room was lit up, the family seated around a big table. If he was hungry he tried to make out what they were eating. During the days he would go into shops, pretending to be *very* interested until a clerk opened up and spent time with him. In the museums he learned local history, and in the art galleries he talked so much about the paintings that the sales attendants were sure he was going to return and buy something.

When he had "used up" a small town, he would go back to the airport and wait again patiently for a pilot who looked lonely. There seemed to be a kind of underground network among pilots. If Phillip mentioned a desired destination, a pilot might say, "I'm not going that way, but I know a man who is."

Phillip knew that he needed to be going to some exact destination, so he would study his map, concentrating on small and middle-sized towns that he could mention with ease.

He visited bars, but he seldom had more than one drink. One bar stands out in his memory above all others. It was somewhere in Texas. He had caught a ride in a Beechcraft and landed at an airfield where the only other planes were Lear jets. At first glance this seemed just like any other airport bar. But the counter proved to be marble, the bar stools of fine leather, with hand-carved designs.

He observed the customers, men in leather boots and blue or gray shirts—obviously millionaires, but trying to look like average Texans. They were being served sandwiches at side-booths by a waitress named Mabel.

It struck him as one of the funniest sights he had ever seen, a high-class bar where everything was aimed at playing down wealth. Those men with their Lear jets joked with Mabel and no doubt left her $100 tips.

This place was the climax of his travels. He could think of no other place he wanted to visit.

He was experiencing *burnout*. He had not eaten regularly for months; sometimes he went a whole night without sleep. He was having headaches. He had lost his drive. When he felt ill there was no one to complain to. He was out of money and did not have the energy to earn more.

At last he found a pilot who was flying to Santa Rosa, near enough to San Francisco so he could get back to one of his friends on Haight Street.

He found his friend, who had a single bed in a small room. Phillip slept on the floor and waited for fate to find him a better place.

Conversation After the Late Show

If *TV Guide* lists a movie I want to see again, I stay up past my bedtime to watch it with Phillip. Most old movies are new to him. One night we watched *Splendor in the Grass* with Warren Beatty. He made me think of Henry Briggs, my first real boyfriend, the summer between junior and senior years of high school in 1925.

Can you imagine Warren Beatty as a farm boy, driving his father's Model T Ford, coming to my door all slicked up and smelling of bay rum and Sen-Sen? My parents were strict and would permit me to go on dates only if it were to the one movie theater in town, and if we didn't stay for the second show.

This restriction caused our dates to be a race against ten o'clock, when the first show was over. We would drive away from my house, heading toward town. After three blocks we turned south from the highway to where several lanes leading nowhere took off from the main road. If a favorite spot was occupied, we went on to find another.

These Lover's Lanes did their best business on Saturday nights.

After the engine stopped and lights were out, Henry would move a few inches closer and say, "How about a little Armstrong Heater?" (Armstrong Heater was the name of a popular brand of heating stove used at that time.) Henry would put his right arm around my shoulder, and I would move a few inches in his direction. His left hand was free, and so the battle began. This was a contest I knew I had to win. I wasn't that kind of girl. But it was great while it lasted, mostly a silent struggle, with an occasional kiss.

46

At that time we had not watched television, so we did not know about French kisses, but now and then there was a little trouble with chewing gum.

It required both my hands to slow the progress of Henry's hands, the left hand going up from the knee and the right going downward, both headed for no-man's-land.

Now and then, the action would stop while Henry looked at his watch to be sure we could meet the ten o'clock deadline. As the zero hour approached, he always asked, "What are you saving it for?"

I never answered. I wasn't sure.

On Sunday morning I would call Mildred Ambecker to get her to tell me the plot of the movie I had missed—so I could give my mother sufficient details. Mildred never had a date, but she went to every movie that came to town.

Through the week I went about in a daze, helping Mama in the garden, taking the two-block walk to the grocery store, getting books from the library—always ones that were on Mama's approved list. Sometimes I sat and practiced my penmanship, the fine Spencerian hand I had learned in the required course for the junior year. I filled pages with "Mr. and Mrs. Henry Briggs," along with push-and-pulls, always using good arm movement. And I waited anxiously for Henry's telephone call. When it finally came, he would always say, "How would you like to go to the show Saturday night?" and I always giggled a little before I asked what time he would pick me up.

Our romance lasted well into August. Then he stopped calling. I knew he had given up.

One Saturday I waited until five o'clock before I called Mildred Ambecker and asked if I could walk to the show with her. I had paid dearly for my victory over Henry. Mildred had bad breath, and she whispered all through the show. She didn't use Sen-Sen.

*   *   *

"I can't match a story like that one," Phillip told me. "I

never ran into many *good* girls. Sometimes it was the other
way round. Did I ever tell you about Lucky?"

He had told me about his favorite whore, Lucky, whom
he'd met in Denver. He had told me about her in October
and in January and in August, but I could hear it again.
She gave him what was probably the biggest thrill of his life.

Most of Phillip's time in Denver was spent away from his
small, lonely room — in libraries or art galleries or restaurants. He fell into what he describes as his *scuffy* time. He
wore sandals without socks and let his hair grow. He even
stopped trimming his beard. He wore black, which made
him look even skinnier than he was. He had enough money
under his mattress for rent and food, so he wasn't really
looking for a job; he more or less just fell into one. He had
been spending a lot of time in a particular art gallery, out
on the edge of the city. Apparently, he had made an impres-
sion on one owner, who one day asked Phillip if he would
like to work through the noon hour and three afternoons a
week. Phillip pretended to think it over before he accepted.

One of those afternoons a woman came into the gallery
alone. She wore a white fur over an elegant black dress and
she sparkled with diamonds. She could have been a society
woman, but instinct told him she was not. She reminded
him of Simone, the "lady of the evening" he had known in
New Orleans.

The owner of the gallery was out to a long lunch, so
Phillip entertained this woman with the best he had to offer
in conversation. He explained the paintings, and showed
off his knowledge of travel and important people. She
made it clear that she knew a few important people, too —
important men, that is.

As she left, Phillip opened the door for her and told her
his name, pronouncing it with a very French accent.

"Just call me Lucky," she replied.

Another afternoon, she arrived in a chauffeured black
Cadillac. Phillip was with a customer, and could only greet
her casually. As she left she told him, "You are a very

interesting man. I'd like to talk with you again. How can I get in touch with you?"

Phillip had no telephone, and he hated giving her the address of his shabby room, so he said, "I'll call you."

She gave him a card with her number scrawled in blue ink. He put it in his pocket.

After a lonely week, it came to him that Lucky might be as lonely for someone to talk to as he was. He kept remembering what Simone had said to him, "I have a large, fancy apartment, but no one to go home to." Lucky might be just as hungry for conversation as Simone had been. Phillip understood people like that. He kept remembering that, as a boy, he had not been allowed to play with other children because his mother considered all the people who lived near their home *peasants*. So he had no friends. He would throw his toys, one by one, out the window of his upstairs room in the hope that the children who found them would like him.

He called Lucky from a phone booth in front of a corner restaurant where he often ate. He told her where he was and hung up. Then he went inside and ordered a beer. The place was crowded. There was loud talking and laughter. The other men were dressed roughly, but none were as *scuffy* as he was. He felt that no one would notice if Lucky didn't show up and he walked out alone. If she failed to come, he could live with it.

Phillip sat with his head bowed, looking into his empty beer mug, trying to decide whether to order another. Then he sensed a silence all around him. He looked up to see that a black Cadillac had stopped out front and a chauffeur was holding the door open. Lucky stepped out and entered the café. Her eyes searched the tables. He was too stunned to get to his feet quickly, but she spotted him and walked over, her heels clicking and her diamonds glittering.

"Hello, Phillip," she said for all to hear.

He got to his feet and followed her. He even strutted a bit. At the door he turned and faced his public. He could not resist making a deep bow before he walked to the Cadillac and allowed himself to be helped into the back seat by the chauffeur.

It was one of the high points of his life. He felt that if he had died the next day, his life would have been worth living.

Lucky took him to her apartment, high above Denver. The thick drapes, the soft rugs, the velvet divan were all very elegant, but a little gaudy. "Very adequate," he said.

She even had a shelf of books. He took down a volume of Shakespeare, opened it, and quoted lines he knew by heart. She answered with another quote, and they were in business. He named the artists whose prints she had on the wall without looking at their signatures.

She never mentioned how she had acquired all her luxury, and he didn't tell her that, at the moment, he was almost penniless. But when she followed him to the door as he left, she pressed a hundred-dollar bill into his hand.

White Shirts and Butter

Phillip has a favorite white shirt that he bought at the Thrift Corner for twenty-five cents. He washes it every Saturday night and lets it drip-dry overnight to wear to church. He comes into the kitchen to ask for soap, and I am reminded of my first husband, Richard, and the early days of our marriage.

Unlike Phillip, Richard had never been a bachelor, so he never thought of washing his own shirts. He graduated straight from his mother to me. My mother-in-law was thin, nervous, and completely devoted to her only son. She had planned all his life for him to go to college and become a doctor. Instead, he married me and became a bookkeeper. He wore white shirts and in summer he needed a new one every day. I was expected to make sure they always looked like new.

The term *drip-dry* had not yet been invented. There weren't even any laundromats. Either you sent clothes to the laundry or you coped with them in your own kitchen. Richard's mother had never been known to send anything to the laundry: They used too much starch and they lost buttons.

Before our wedding she told me exactly how to do Richard's shirts. He liked plenty of starch in the collar and down the front and cuffs, with only a little stiffness in the sleeves and back. I was to use only a little blueing, enough to keep the shirts from looking yellow, but not too much, or it would make streaks. The shirts were to be boiled, but I must be careful never to let a white shirt touch one of my colored dresses, or I would have a spot.

51

Then, before hanging the shirts to dry, I must carefully clean the clothesline with a damp cloth. I was to bring the shirts into the house before they were quite dry, roll them carefully, and put them in the laundry basket.

Then came the ironing, no later than the next day. I was to work rapidly, doing the starched parts first and then the sleeves and back. If I was too slow, the backs of the shirts would turn out wrinkled.

I was never quite fast enough. My shirts looked unhappy on their hangers, and so did Richard's face when he saw them.

Our wedding and honeymoon took place in late May, after my school was out, so that I had the three summer months to get the curtains up, learn to cook what Richard liked to eat, and master the laundry problem. I had no washing machine, so I used a big copper boiler and a washtub. Ring around the collar was handled on the rub-board.

I felt a bit guilty about continuing to teach after I was married. Since Richard had a good job, with a salary of $110 a month, there were some who thought I should stay home and give my job to some deserving young woman with no husband to support her. But I was determined to go back to my second graders and show everyone, especially the school board, that I could still be a good teacher, even if I was married.

The Saturday of Labor Day weekend, with school to start in three days, I washed my clothes, rolled them up, put them in the clothes basket, and forgot about them.

The first week of school was exciting. Friday afternoon I was ready to celebrate. I stopped at the grocery store on my way home and bought two pork chops, a tomato, and a pint of ice cream. (We had only an icebox, no electric refrigerator, so my plan was to eat the whole pint that night.)

My first shock on coming home was the sight and smell of steam. My copper boiler was across three burners of the stove. My slim, neat mother-in-law was scrubbing at the hamburger grease spots I had meant to clean off the wall.

My father-in-law stood in the doorway, looking apologetic. "I tried to get her just to sit here in the living room until you got home," he said. "I wanted her to call before we came, but she had it in her head to surprise you."

She kept on scrubbing. "I know how it is when girls get married before they know how to keep house," she said. "I knew you'd be teaching this week and I thought you could use a little help. It's a good thing, too, because mildew had set in on Richard's shirts. I had to wash them before I could boil them."

I set my ice cream on the kitchen table and stood there, taking deep breaths to hold my temper. I went into the dining room and saw that two of Richard's colored, everyday shirts were draped across a chair. They had been hanging in the closet.

"I found those two shirts that need buttons," my mother-in-law called to me. "But I couldn't find your button box."

"I don't have one," I admitted. "I haven't been married long enough."

I heard Richard's car pulling into the garage, and waited for him to enter the back door. He took in the situation at a glance. He kissed his mother, greeted his father, and shook his head sadly at me. Then he rescued the pint of ice cream from the kitchen table, put the pork chops away, turned out the burners from the boiler, and took us all to dinner — or to supper — at the café down across from the place where he worked.

He was very silent that night after his parents had left. He said, "She meant well."

Now, after fifty years, this once painful memory sends Phillip and me into gales of laughter — too late to help the woman I was, but awfully good for the one I am.

* * *

"I used to iron my shirts, too," Phillip said. "I bought

myself an iron when I decided for sure that I was going to
be a bachelor all my life. I knew I had to learn to take care
of my clothes and do my own cooking. I wanted to learn to
take care of myself without a woman."

He had met a very nice woman who spoke with a French
accent and found out that she owned a hotel in San Francisco's North Beach. The rent was no problem because, at
this particular time in his life, Phillip was enjoying an
inheritance from an uncle who had never married. He
located a French restaurant where his favorite French
dishes were served, and by tipping the cook and showering
him with compliments, he learned exactly how to make his
favorite — *coq au vin,* a chicken dish with wine.

In North Beach, Phillip created his own existence, sepa-
rate from the rest of the world. "I kept the shades drawn so
I didn't know night from day. To me, anyone who wore a
wristwatch and kept looking at it was common. I ate when I
was hungry and slept when I was sleepy — I created my own
time."

It was such an effortless life that he did not want to
interrupt it with a search for work. He still did not use a
bank, but continued to keep his money under the mattress.
After several weeks, he was shocked to find that the bills in
the little leather bag were almost gone. That week he did
not pay his rent and the kind landlady did not mention it.
Phillip knew that somehow he must eat, whether the rent
was paid or not, so he bought some rice, cheese, and bread.
To cook the rice he found a small kettle with a lid. He
smuggled everything up the back stairway, avoiding the
landlady because he knew it was against the rules to cook in
the rooms.

For a time he ate one meal a day at the restaurant and
signed for it, with a promise to pay at the end of the week.
Being a Frenchman, the owner accepted the tickets with a
nod and a smile, which grew a little thin by the end of two
weeks.

Phillip still had a few dollars left when he recalled his directions for making *coq au vin*. He bought a small chicken and cooked it slowly on a stove he rigged up by laying a chair on its side and securing his electric iron between two rungs. It took nearly all day to cook the chicken so that it was tender enough to pick from the bones. Next he added mushrooms, sharp green olives, onions, tomato paste, and the last of his bottle of red wine. With a big spoon he had bought for a nickel at the Thrift Store, he planned to eat directly from the pan. He had just taken the first bite when he heard a sharp tap on the door. He opened it to see his landlady standing there with her mouth half open.

Instead of reprimanding him, she said, "I thought I smelled coq au vin!" She walked over and looked into the pot. He gave her the spoon. She took a big portion and swallowed it slowly. "That's the best I ever ate," she said. She did not say one word about his rent being past due or breaking the rules by cooking in his room.

He was so grateful to her that he resolved to go out and try to get a job. But while he looked, he had to eat. He managed this in several ways.

One way was to talk up the service and the fine food of the French restaurant to tourists he happened to meet. One couple seemed so prosperous that he offered to go along with them and help them order the best food served. Of course he felt very sure they would pay the bill. He washed out his white shirt and pressed his tie and trimmed his Vandyke carefully, so that he looked his best.

The meal was excellent and the couple was truly grateful. As he had hoped, they paid the bill. Then, to his horror, as they stood to leave, the man placed a twenty-dollar bill on the table as a tip. This was the temptation of his life. He could see food for a week in the money they were giving away. Suddenly, with shame and guilt, he pretended to have lost something under his chair. With nimble fingers he rescued the money and joined his friends.

"That was very sharp of you," I said. "But twenty dollars couldn't last forever."

"I gave plasma."

"You mean you were a blood donor?"

"No," he answered. "Giving plasma is much worse. You let them take out your blood, then they put it through some kind of a process and then return it to you—ice cold. They pay a flat rate of five dollars. It takes three hours and it hurts. You only go through that if you're very hungry."

"How did you spend the five dollars?" I asked.

"I bought one pound of butter and a lot of rice," he said. "The butter ran out before the rice. I had no money, but there was a grocery store right across the street. I decided to walk through, pretending to be a shopper. When I thought no one was looking I took just one quarter of a pound of butter. I was almost to the door when the owner of the store walked up behind me and told me if I ever came into the place again he would have me arrested. I walked straight ahead, pretending not to hear him, but I never did go back there again. All that shame for a quarter of a pound of butter."

"Why did you have to steal butter? Why not margarine?"

We could both laugh at that because learning to live with Phillip's ideas of food was a big part of my learning to *put up* with him. He was unbending. He considered margarine in the class with Wonder Bread and part-skim cheese. He was also against fish sticks and frozen French fries and TV dinners. If I served any of those things he simply did not eat—at least after that first week he came to me. At first, he ate anything. He bragged that he was once so hungry he ate a can of cat food.

"It wasn't too bad," he said.

Rented Rooms

I often find it interesting to talk to Phillip about the way things were before he was born. One day he got my blue trunk down from the top of my closet, and I took out the photographs I'm saving to give to my grandchildren some day. One was of a large white house with a porch all around the lower story and a dormer window on the corner. "This is where I lived for two years in Wichita," I told him. "It had five bedrooms upstairs, but only one bathroom in the whole ten rooms."

"I lived in a house like that in San Francisco," he said, "you could almost call it a mansion, but it had only one bathroom. Why was that?"

"Because in the days when it was built every bedroom had a washbowl and pitcher on the dresser and a slop jar to pour the water in. There was always a little chamber pot to go under the foot of the bed."

Richard and three-year-old Karen and I had moved to Wichita near the end of the Great Depression. We didn't consider ourselves Okies. They headed for California in old jalopies. Richard was such a good bookkeeper that he was offered a place in a wholesale house at a salary of $85 a month. So we put a For Sale sign on our five-room house in Hammon, the small town where we had lived for five years, and moved to Wichita.

For a time we existed in a two-room furnished apartment. Every morning I listened to "Ma Perkins" and "Stella Dallas" on the radio. Every afternoon I took Karen for a walk and watched for some house with a For Rent sign. But every time I found one and asked about the rent, it was beyond us.

Then I discovered an item that interested me in the income property column of the newspaper. I bundled Karen into her jacket and leggings and we took the bus. The place was very near the downtown area. My spirits fell when I saw how dilapidated it was, with peeling paint and rickety steps, but Karen spotted a sandbox and swing to the side and ran toward it.

A plump older woman came to the door as Karen and I stepped up onto the porch.

"We've come to find out about the income property," I said.

"I'm Sally Reed," she said. "I'm keeping the place up for the owners. They don't pay me anything, but I get the use of the downstairs. The rent for you is fifty dollars, but you have four renters upstairs; they pay thirty for the two rooms in front—a married couple lives there—and twenty for the singles. You can earn your rent and set by a little extra."

Directly behind her was a large white refrigerator, the kind with an electric unit sticking out on top. She opened the door so I could look inside.

"It's the only one in the house," she said. "I keep it here in the hall so the renters can all keep their milk cold and their butter from melting."

We walked through the living room. There was a double bed in the parlor. "There's no closets," Mrs. Reed told us. She pulled aside a curtain draped across a corner of the room. "You can put the little girl on the couch in the living room. The kitchen is large and sunny. You can do most of your living in here," she added.

Karen and I followed Mrs. Reed up the steps. She knocked on a closed door. We heard a muffled, "Yes."

"That's Mrs. Holman in there," the landlady explained. "She cries a lot since her husband died, and she's constipated."

The door opened and Mrs. Holman rushed out without meeting our eyes.

The bathroom was large, with a huge white tub on claws. Mrs. Reed put her hand on the hot water tank in the corner. "I tell people not to fill up the tub when they take their baths," she said. "I advise them to take their baths in the evening when they don't have to rush."

That night as soon as supper was over the three of us returned to make up our minds about the place. Richard's face dropped when he saw the neglected yard, but he smiled when he saw the sandbox and swing. "I guess it'll look better in the spring," he said. He kicked at the dry dirt by the porch. "I won't mind a little yard work."

We moved in the next week, and Mrs. Reed introduced me to the renters. The Strattons came home from work together and stopped at the refrigerator to get their butter and milk. He had a sack of groceries. Both were tall, he with dark hair and she with a short red bob. She called to me as she hurried up the steps, "Let's have a nice talk tomorrow. I'm starved now."

Mrs. Reed took me up to the back room and knocked on Mr. Jennings's door. It opened slowly. He stood there, leaning a little, his face lined and his thin hair uncombed. Beyond him I could see a table with a coffee pot and toaster. His bed was unmade and a walking-stick leaned against a chair. He stuck out his hand. His grip was stronger than I expected. I looked straight into his eyes and I saw kindness and patience.

We went on to Mrs. Holman's door. We could hear her sobbing. "I'll see her tomorrow," I said.

There was another door just before the bathroom door, but we passed it. The next day, as I walked by, it was ajar. I thought it must be a storage room, so I opened it. Sitting on a single bed was a young woman, very pregnant. She wore a skimpy blue print dress. Her face looked flushed. "Are you ill?" I asked. She managed her name, Bertha, and then she began to cry again. "I can't pay any rent," she said.

"Mrs. Reed gave me leftovers sometimes, and she bought me milk."

In the days that followed I invited Bertha for lunch every day. I forced vegetables on her whether she wanted them or not. I learned that Mr. Jennings bought a loaf of bread every week and that was all he ate except for going out every afternoon about four o'clock and eating at the place down the street that had a sign in the window saying, *All You Can Eat for a Quarter*. I took him a glass of homemade jelly to use on his toast.

The walls were thin and almost every night I could hear the Strattons' angry voices. Now and then I heard noises up there at the noon hour. One day Mr. Stratton asked me if his wife had come home at noon and if she had had anyone with her.

Another time Mrs. Stratton asked me the same question about her husband. I said I hadn't noticed.

Mr. Stratton complained that he was late to work because Mrs. Holman stayed in the bathroom too long . . .

Mrs. Stratton complained that someone was using her butter from the refrigerator . . .

Bertha and Mr. Jennings and Mrs. Holman never complained about anything. When I went into Mr. Jennings's room to vacuum, I saw his soiled shirt and shorts on the chair. I asked if he would like me to do his laundry along with mine. He protested, but I insisted. I had no dryer, so I hung the clothes on the line. That night Richard was very upset to see Mr. Jennings's blue-striped shorts hanging next to his.

Mr. Jennings showed me a German helmet he'd taken from a dead soldier. He also had a tattered wallet that he'd picked up after seeing a soldier blown to pieces. It was full of family pictures, and it had an address in Tennessee. He had always meant to let those people know that their boy had suffered no pain. Now, almost twenty years after the war had ended, I told him I'd relay his message.

I asked Bertha to take Karen for a walk every day. That way both of them got out in the fresh air. I heard about a creative writing course offered at the library and asked Bertha to babysit.

My first story was about her. It told how she was the daughter of a Methodist minister, and how she'd gone out with this man who said he was in love with her until she told him she was expecting a baby. Then he left town. She couldn't ask her father for help, because he would be ashamed of her. So she stayed in this little room, rent free, and had very little food while she waited for the baby.

The teacher told the class, "I think we might have the makings of a story here." But the trouble was, I couldn't think up a good ending.

One story, which I didn't read to the writing class, I called "The Man Upstairs." I mailed it to *True Story* magazine. Part of my story was the truth, the part about how Mr. Jennings had returned from the war and his wife didn't want him anymore. She married another man, who wouldn't let him see his own children. Now he lived in an upstairs room and ate toast all day. I also included some sex and some fantasy, because all the stories printed in *True Story* had a little of that to make them interesting.

The story came back with a rejection slip the week I had taken Karen to see her grandmother in Oklahoma. When we got home, Richard didn't seem very glad to see me. I didn't understand until I saw the large brown envelope already opened. I tried to explain the requirements of a *True Story* story, how it had to have some sex and fantasy. But not being a writer, he couldn't understand.

One day a tall, serious man in a gray suit knocked at my door. He asked if his daughter Bertha lived here. My first instinct was to turn and tell Bertha to run and hide, but she was standing back of me, in sight. She ran, crying, to her father's arms. He embraced her with tears in his eyes. There was not one bit of shame or blame in his face. One of her letters must have let him guess her condition. My story made up an ending of its own, a good one.

Bertha's father waited while she packed her few things, and he carried her suitcase to his car.

Mrs. Holman finally got a job as a clerk in a department store downtown. She finished up in the bathroom early so she could catch the bus.

The Strattons put a down payment on a house on the outskirts of town, even though it was so far out they wouldn't be able to come home at noon . . .

I put up a *For Rent* sign. I had to find new renters.

Mr. Jennings had such pains in his legs that he had to go to the Veteran's Hospital. I went to visit him on Thursdays, when Karen went to nursery school. Some of the other men had visitors, but none except me ever came to see Mr. Jennings on Thursdays. I reached out and held his hand. His fingers were strong, even though he looked weak and pale.

He told me he loved me.

Change of Pace

The memory of World War II and the words *War Effort* bring different pictures to my mind than to Phillip's. To him, war is the whistle of bombs overhead. To me, it is the time when the shadow of the Great Depression was lifted.

The tempo of Wichita quickened as the Boeing aircraft plant began to go up. People from out of state in old cars, loaded down with family possessions, could be seen driving slowly along the streets, looking for places to live. They often stopped where there were no *For Rent* signs and begged to be given just a room or a garage to rent.

Our family life changed, too. When we knew for sure that Lenni was on the way, Richard made plans to move from the big white house and find us a home of our own. We had saved enough for a down payment on a $2500 house. It had a basement and garage, with five rooms downstairs and an upstairs bedroom. We soon rented the garage to a couple from Arkansas. Mama came from Oklahoma to live upstairs and be with us when Lenni was born.

I considered this sharing of our new home as my war effort, though Richard complained when he had to stand outside the bathroom waiting to shave.

By the time Lenni was six months old, I was in a fever to locate my birth certificate so I could apply for a job at Boeing along with almost everyone else I knew. Mama loved the girls and it made her feel useful to the war effort to offer to stay and care for them while I worked. To get a job at Boeing for a salary of $1.20 an hour, I went early one morning and stayed the whole day for tests. Because I had been a teacher for five years they told me I could qualify as a timekeeper. I chose the swing shift, going to work at three in the afternoon and getting off at eleven at night. I missed sitting around the dinner table and going to movies and seeing Karen come home from school, but I was able to enjoy taking Lenni for a daily trip in her baby carriage.

I soon became involved in a world that centered around the building of the giant B-29s. The riveting was deafening, but I soon learned to lip-read. I became not so much a timekeeper as a public relations person. While the riveters had to stay in one spot for hours, I moved about and carried news. I would say, "See the man at the far end? He told me he has nine children and is expecting another one. He's from Arkansas."

They would remember and ask, "Has the baby come yet?"

We women all dressed alike in dark pants and shirts with our hair completely covered by scarfs that tied in front with a knot. It was the first time I'd worn pants, except for picnics. We were a kind of home-front army, making instant friends.

"I watch for your smile every day," a man told me.

Often a toolbox would be opened to reveal a sack of lemon drops. I would take one and it would be a bond between us. So many times a hand reached out to touch. We were all on a kind of *high*.

It was not that we did not feel the tragedy of the war that had freed us from the Great Depression. I said, "See the girl in the red scarf? She got word that her brother was killed, but here she is *today*, working as usual." Then my job was to carry the love and sympathy to her on my next time around.

Because of the noise we were drawn together with a kind of body language. The touch of a hand on my arm, the wink, the smile, the hand grabbed and kissed, the pinch on the rear when no one was looking—all combined to give me such a high that it was hard to go to sleep when I got home to the calmness of a life with two children, a husband, and a mother.

For the first time in my life I was in contact with many men. I got an idea for a magazine article. I called it, "Can War Workers Go Back to One Man?" I sent along a picture of myself with my pad and pencil. I was leaning against a B-29, looking up at a man who was smiling at me. One of the men had brought a camera in his toolbox and taken the picture.

Because the article was timely, it sold on the first trip out to a magazine called *She*, which is no longer published. In three months it was on the newsstands. I didn't really intend for Richard and Mama to see it, but my vanity got the better of me and I left a copy of the magazine on the library table.

Mama read the article first. I saw in her face the pride she always felt that her daughter was a talented person, capable of writing something that would be published, but shame that she had chosen *that* subject.

Richard did not meet my eyes as he finished reading the article. Lenni toddled across the room and pulled at his leg. He picked her up and held her in his arms. I walked to the window and looked out at the side yard. Richard had planted flowers and they were now in full bloom, but I hadn't noticed. The high I had been on for all those months had separated me from my home and family.

Mama and Karen came into the kitchen, each carrying a basket of clothes from the lines out back. I hadn't hung out any clothes for a long time. Mama had taken over all my small jobs. I turned to her and asked, "If I quit my job would you like to go back to Oklahoma and see your sisters?"

I saw the knowing look come to her face. "I *am* getting a little homesick," she said. "I ought to go see how my yard is doing. It's probably all grown up in weeds."

It was not hard to resign from Boeing, new people were hired every day. For a while my daily routine of getting

Karen off to school, bathing Lenni and taking her for her walk, and having dinner on the table when Richard got home was enough.

It was the HELP WANTED ads in the Wichita *Beacon* that lured me. Not only the aircraft plants needed help; jobs were available downtown too. I tried to fill my time with PTA meetings, the Tuesday-Night Poetry Center, my Writing-to-Sell class at the library, family picnics, and weekly movies, but everyone I knew seemed to be earning money and buying things. Having only Richard's salary as a bookkeeper, we were again pinching pennies.

A neighbor with two little girls of her own often looked after Lenni. One morning I put together a folder of the few things I had had published. Most of them were to church school publications, but I did have my article in *She* and two short stories in *Family Circle*. I took Lenni to her baby-sitter, three doors down the block, and headed for the Wichita *Beacon* office. In no time at all I was hired as a replacement for a reporter who had gone to Boeing. Before I told Richard, I made arrangements for the neighbor to spend days at our place, bringing along her two small girls.

Richard's face looked grim when I told him I was going to work away from home again, but he knew we needed the money.

By working days I was able to be with my family more. Very quickly I was able to master the who, what, where, and when of the lead paragraph. I interviewed servicemen and rewrote news releases from overseas; this was now *my* "war effort." I became church editor and got a box of chocolates from the Methodist minister. I made the front page and a by-line when I interviewed the head of the Mormon church and started my article off with a statement that members of that church were even stricter about marriage vows to one mate than members of other denominations. I was sent a large box of Utah celery, packed in ice, to share with the others in the office. I went with the photographer to a fire and was able to phone in all the facts, just like reporters in the movies.

I began to dream of working in a newspaper office for the rest of my life. I would go down in history as one of the top women reporters.

The week before Thanksgiving Mama returned to spend the holidays with us. She took over all the household duties, which left me free time. I used the extra hours to try for more by-lines. We got the first Christmas tree on the block, and Richard placed it near the front window so that those going past the house could see the blue lights, the strings of popcorn, and the white clad angel that Grandma made from a little naked doll. Then began the making and wrapping of the gifts.

The home celebration was to start on Christmas Eve, with black-eyed peas, because that was what Mary was supposed to have eaten when Christ was born. Then we would have stewed chicken and dumplings, the dish we'd had since I was a small child. This time Mama didn't have to go kill the chicken, as she'd done when we lived on a farm in the Ozarks.

Preparations were going on at the newspaper office, too. The secretary to the editor put up red streamers and brought a tablecloth for the front desk. The men brought bottles and hid them in their desks. The office party was to begin when we finished turning in our material for the Christmas edition. (We all worked late the day before.) I wore my eighty-dollar dress — not that it cost that much; it was on sale half-price. It was made of clinging black crepe with a beaded front and shoulder pads, so that I felt a little like Joan Crawford. As I took off my coat and entered the office, somebody whistled.

An office party was something I had read about, but never experienced. No one went out for lunch. We all abandoned our typewriters and ate cheese-topped crackers and homemade cookies supplied by the wives of the staff.

Along with the food we drank wine from the bottles that had been hidden. We forgot all about the passing of time. The two other women on the staff were busy making more sandwiches in the back office. For the first time in my life I was sitting on top of a desk, with my legs crossed. The photographer, the sports editor, and the proofreader were leaning against the desk. We were all laughing.

Suddenly I felt a silence in the room. My eyes went to the opened door at the head of the stairs. Richard stood there with six-year-old Karen and two-year-old Lenni, both in their winter coats and knitted caps. They had been begging to see the place where Mama worked and now they were seeing it.

"Grandma is waiting supper," Richard said.

I put my wine glass down and hurried into the hallway to get my coat. We went down the stairs, walked silently to where the car was parked, and rode through the streets of Wichita toward home. The Christmas lights blinked at us through the early twilight. A little snow had fallen through the afternoon.

Grandma was watching for us so she could open the door. "I'll go warm up the dumplings," she said. She was wearing her flowered silk dress and her comb with sparklers.

The two girls took off their coats to show me their twin dresses, red for Christmas, that Grandma had made to surprise me.

When we finished eating, we opened the gifts.

Richard and I put on a good show. We shook our gift packages and laughed a lot, but when we were alone in the bedroom, we were very silent. The newspaper office was closed for the holiday, but when we went to clear out my desk the next day, I knocked on the door until the janitor came and unlocked it for us.

Mama told us that she needed to return to Oklahoma and see about her sisters.

I began to talk about how I would like to go out to California. Richard admitted that he had never really liked living in Wichita; the place was too big and noisy. He said we should sell our home while we could get a good price for it. We did sell it for double what we had paid, and we had enough money to buy a house trailer and put $4000 in the bank. We had never been so rich.

"We weren't sorry to leave Wichita," I told Phillip. "We were like you, we had *used up* the place."

Amazing Grace

I never sit beside Phillip at church. We arrive together, but then I go sit with my women friends, most of them widows too. I hope that he will find someone interesting to sit with, and he always manages. This is one of the differences between the two of us and the married couples.

By the time the service starts, there is an electricity between us that tells me exactly where he is sitting. For one thing, he puts something extra into his singing, so that I hear him, apart from the other voices. Once, during the second verse of "Amazing Grace," everyone around me stopped singing altogether in order to listen to Phillip. At the words, "that saved a wretch like me," his voice was pure feeling. The woman beside me seemed near tears.

That night I said to him, "I thought you grew up a Catholic and only went to mass when it suited you. When did you learn these Protestant songs?"

He avoided the question, as if he were ashamed, but I continued to wonder about other things, such as how he happened to know more about the Bible than I did, though I had taught Sunday School classes for twenty years.

We always go into the social hall after services, and Phillip makes a point of greeting new members and visitors. He always seems to know something about wherever they may have lived before—a special building, a river running through the town, a nearby college or monastery.

The third or fourth time this happened, I thought for sure he must have psychic powers. How else could he know so much about Mobile, Alabama, and Grand Forks, North

Dakota? I could understand Chicago and New Orleans and
Denver, but small towns seemed out of keeping . . .

The answer became clear one night after we had watched
All About Eve on TV. I wanted to discuss Anne Baxter and
Bette Davis, but Phillip got up from his place on the couch
and began going in circles around the room, in what I call
his caged mood.

"George Sanders reminds me so much of a man I used to
know named Larry Bronson," he said. "He has that same
style and charm. Women go for that, you know."

I had to laugh. "From the stories you've told me," I said,
"the same thing could be said of you."

"It's different with me," Phillip answered. "I have to put
out. Larry didn't have to do anything. He was just there. I
think it's the maternal instinct that makes some women like
me — maybe a little too much sometimes — but with Larry it
is just plain desire. One side of his face was slightly para-
lyzed, but it made him attractive, if you can believe that."

Phillip sat down on the couch beside me, with just
enough distance so he could look me straight in the eyes.
"You asked me once how I know the songs at church and so
much about the small towns all over the United States?
How I could have been so many places at my age. I've held
off telling you, I guess, because I was a little bit ashamed.
Have you ever gone door-to-door?"

"I was an Avon Lady for over a year," I answered.

It was plain that Phillip was not interested in my adventures as an Avon Lady. He got up again and started pacing.
He was full of the story of himself and Larry and ready to
talk about it.

"Where did you meet this man?"

He had just paid his hotel bill, Phillip explained, and was
feeling in his pocket to see if he had enough change left for
a breakfast of bacon and eggs, or if he would have to make
do with a cup of coffee and a doughnut, when he saw that
the man beside him was trying to fit a thick roll of bills back
into his wallet.

Phillip turned away and looked out toward the street. A porter was putting two suitcases into the trunk of a maroon Cadillac convertible. It had New York license plates. Phillip took his own suitcase out and put it down next to the Cadillac.

When the man with the wallet walked up to the car, Phillip asked if he could have a ride to New York.

The man looked at him closely, then told him to put his suitcase in the back.

They went to New York the long way.

As they drove, Phillip managed to convey to Larry that he was a bit down on his luck, that he was from an important background, that he knew a great deal about art and literature, and that he spoke French better than English.

All this before Larry stopped the car in front of a restaurant in a small town and they went in for lunch. There Larry revealed that he was in the business of selling magazine subscriptions. If Phillip wanted to make a little money, he would show him how it was done.

Selling magazine subscriptions was not exactly what Phillip had planned for his life, but he had skipped breakfast and by now he was hungry.

Larry ordered steak for both of them, and even a glass of wine. He tipped the waitress with a five-dollar bill. She was so grateful that she hovered about, neglecting her other customers. This was Phillip's first lesson in selling magazines. In a few minutes the waitress had told Larry the names of the banker, the doctor, and the richest widow in town. Larry explained that recent widows were his best prospects, because they usually felt guilty about all that insurance . . . and would often take five-year subscriptions!

Larry looked up the banker's address in the phone book. They found the street, and finally the house. As they walked up to the front door, Larry cautioned Phillip to speak only in French, and to be careful what he said, as someone might know the language.

A fat, pleasant-faced woman answered the door. Larry explained that Phillip needed just a few more magazine subscriptions before he could return to Paris to visit his mother, who was mortally ill. The woman believed the story, bought two subscriptions, and smiled as Phillip thanked her profusely and even kissed her hand.

Then they drove to a small park. Larry spread a map out on a picnic table. He put an X on the town where they were. "I might stop here again," he said. "But for now I want to go on to some larger place where we can find a good hotel." He pointed to a town that looked to be only an hour away. "There's a monastery here," he said. "Nuns have lots of money hidden away. Don't you ever believe they're all poor."

He took a hundred-dollar bill from his wallet and showed it to Phillip. He creased the bill and handed it to him. "Remember, money is the only thing that counts. Keep this for an emergency. You can lie, steal, and cheat, but send in the name and address of every subscriber. What the magazines want are names; they make their money from advertising."

Phillip wondered about this, but he was glad he could keep the money.

Larry explained to him that every town had its *power* people. "One place you can meet them is at church," he said. "Every time we stay in a place on Sunday we will go to the biggest and richest church in town."

Larry also explained that he was married. "I don't see my wife very often," he admitted. "She lives in Nebraska on a farm with her parents. We can make it there for Thanksgiving dinner." Larry looked closely at Phillip. "Have you ever been married?"

Phillip said that he had never gotten that far.

As they drove from town to town, Larry amused himself by telling about his conquests. Phillip never learned to tell the difference between the lies and the truth. All he knew for sure was that they stopped at the best hotels, and they never shared a room. A few times he happened to see one of their customers in the hall, and once a woman knocked on *his* door by mistake, blushing and saying hastily that she thought it was Larry's room.

Phillip pretended to believe all the stories, while not sharing any tales of his own conquests, which in any case seemed tame beside Larry's.

As they traveled north toward Nebraska and Larry's wife, the map was constantly out. Some towns were marked with a big black dot. That meant they were not to stop, but were to drive through. Larry barely kept to the speed limit through those towns. They were places where he had had some unhappy experience with a woman, usually a married one.

At Thanksgiving, as Larry had promised, they neared the farm community where Katy Bronson, Larry's wife, lived with her parents.

As they drove into the yard of a prosperous-looking farm with a tall white house at the end of a long lane, Larry began to look uncomfortable. He said to Phillip, "Don't believe anything these people tell you about me." Two husky young men walked along the road that led from the barn. "Her brothers," Larry explained. Before he and Phillip reached the front door they were met by a joyful woman who ran to Larry and threw her arms around him. Her face, as she looked over Larry's shoulder, was full of love. She wore a simple cotton dress and her brown hair hung loose around her shoulders. She seemed to Phillip very young and vulnerable.

Katy's parents came from the kitchen and the two brothers joined them for introductions. The mother was tall and sober-faced, but the father seemed more friendly. He was gray-haired and dumpy. The brothers both wore bib overalls and were so tall and muscular that Phillip felt small beside them. The mother went ahead of Phillip to show him his room at the top of the stairs. She stood watching as he turned to thank her. "You look like a nice young man," she said. "What are you doing with a man like Larry?"

"I'm eating," Phillip answered.

That brought a reluctant smile to the woman's face. She hurried back downstairs. When he had freshened his face with cold water from the washbasin on his marble-topped dresser, he followed and went into the kitchen, where the smell of mincemeat made him long for the Thanksgiving feast the next day. Larry and Katy seemed to have vanished, no doubt to her bedroom, he thought.

They stayed three days with Katy, her parents, and her two brothers. It was Phillip's first experience on a farm, and he was eager to learn all he could about crops and prices and equipment. This was to serve him well when he went into farm communities to sell magazines.

To Phillip's amazement, Larry's wife decided to go on the road with them. She said it would be like a vacation for her. While she shared Larry's hotel room at night, he told her he needed the time after dinner for totaling up sales and interviewing customers. It became Phillip's lot to sit downstairs in the lobby with Katy and listen for hours as she talked to him about her dreams of the future—a house and babies.

Phillip knew that she often cried herself to sleep. After three weeks, she kissed the two men good-bye and took the bus back to Nebraska.

Phillip stayed on the road with Larry for two whole years. "What made you leave him?" I asked. "Weren't you making much money?"

"It was good money," he replied. "I had good clothes and plenty to eat and we always stayed at the best hotels. I'll tell you what happened that made me take off.

"We were in a small town outside Kansas City, sitting in the hotel lobby, looking at the map. A young woman came into the hotel with a little girl about six years old. She looked around until she saw us sitting there. Larry got up and welcomed her. He told me she had forgotten to order a magazine that she wanted, invited her up to his room, and told me to watch the little girl.

"When the doors to the elevator opened, Larry turned around and *winked* at me."

It was that wink that set Phillip off, he said; it was so *knowing*.

He caught a bus that night back to Kansas City, where he bought a ticket to Denver.

I Have a Place

The word "home" means different things to Phillip and me. In the late sixties, feelings against the Vietnam war ran high and many young people flocked to San Francisco. Phillip knew that if it had not been for the kindness of his French landlady in North Beach, Elizabeth, he might have been sleeping in abandoned buildings and doorways as he saw others doing every night. Yet in other parts of San Francisco there were many large older houses standing vacant. He thought of a plan to get homeless people and old houses together, a plan that would also give him some extra money so he could pay his back rent.

Phillip decided to rent a house and then let out rooms or floorspace, if the rooms ran out. He found just the right house on Fillmore, and learned from the owner that it would cost $200 to get the key and have the utilities turned on. Now all he lacked was the money, which he planned to get from prospective tenants. He spent a week finding just the right people, all of them what he termed *straight*. One was a German exchange student who wasn't ready to leave America. Another was a published poet, unable to make a living from words but giving them away freely to anyone who would listen. Phillip also found a young, unwed mother-to-be who hated staying in the shelter provided for her.

He talked to four musicians who welcomed a place big enough to live and also store their instruments. He found an older woman with a suitcase and two bags sitting on a curb, and he promised her a home even if she didn't have the twenty dollars. He wanted a mix of people.

The day he got the key and let them all inside, it was like a party. The place was barren to begin with, but not for long. Furniture and bedding began to come in from Goodwill, the Salvation Army, abandoned buildings, and alleyways. A big cook stove was already in the kitchen; what they needed was food. That also began to flow in. They cooked together and ate together.

Phillip's motto was, *If I Have a Place, You Have a Place*. He made it work. He always had enough from under the mattress for the monthly rent. If he found himself with a house full of hungry people, he went out and bought rice.

A lot of free love went on in that building. Phillip admitted with a grin that since he was the landlord, he was the prize. It was more than just a summer of love. He said that he had enough love in those days to last a lifetime.

One night Phillip turned off the lights in the big front living room but forgot to lock the front door. A robber sneaked in to lift the silverware or whatever else he could find. As he started to creep silently across the floor, his feet encountered bodies. They heard him curse and mutter, "Man, what the hell is this?" Somebody turned on the lights. Three of Phillip's male tenants grabbed him and shoved him out the front door.

Only now and then did Phillip's idealism get a bit tarnished. He felt sorry for two forlorn-looking girls, runaways from someplace in the Midwest. They had been sleeping outside under a stairway and a policeman had told them about Phillip's place. He gave them two blankets from his own bed and slept cold, with only his coat over him. In the morning, he heard a noise downstairs and found them leaving with his stereo. He unlocked the front door and sent them out into the cold — and didn't feel one bit sorry.

Phillip had no racial prejudice. It simply happened that, while there were many black people in the neighborhood, they never gathered at his place. They were friendly, though, and they accepted him and his renters because the people at Phillip's house had heart and were not like other white people.

All that changed on the day of Martin Luther King's assassination. When the news broke, it was like a declaration of war. Phillip and the others stayed in the house all day, watching the street as blacks congregated in small, angry groups. Those at the window were suddenly horrified to see a white man prone on the sidewalk with a large black man standing over him gouging at his eyes with a linoleum knife.

Phillip let out a yell. He and three men who were watching with him ran out into the street and dragged the injured man into the house. They sent for the ambulance, and when it came the blacks scattered.

Phillip rode in the ambulance and stayed with the man all that night to be sure he lived.

The next day, he returned to find that his renters had gone and taken most of the furniture. He raced upstairs and found that his bed was still there. He felt under the mattress and brought out the little leather bag that held his money—almost $300. That was enough to carry out the plan that had been forming in his mind all night.

The money meant freedom to get away from people. He was suddenly fed up with humans. He longed to be alone. He wanted to prove to himself that he could survive if there were no one else in his life.

He was almost afraid to go out of the house. The faces of the black men and women, friendly until yesterday, had turned stony cold and hostile. Before going out, he waited beside his door, watching until the street seemed fairly clear. Then he hurried away to gather the things he needed for his experiment.

Phillip knew a rich man who owned several hundred acres of land above Bodega Bay, north of San Francisco. He got permission to build himself a small house. Together they went in the man's station wagon to select a spot near a clear stream from which the ocean could be seen. The land was level enough for a house and a garden. It was half a mile off the highway, not visible from any town or other house. It took two more trips in the station wagon to bring all the things Phillip would need.

As the car pulled away, leaving Phillip completely alone, with not even a dog or cat, he resolved not to ask help from anyone. He had been gregarious to the extreme; now he wanted to be alone.

He slept in the open while he built the little house. It had no floor. It was large enough only for his single cot, a black, flat-topped wood stove, a small table, and one chair. He made a shelf for his books.

Being so near the ocean, the weather was warm, and Phillip knew that he could grow vegetables the year around. He brought tomato plants and seed potatoes, along with packets of seeds for other vegetables. Instead of a garden hoe, he used a metal claw to dig up the dirt, and brought it in each night to use for a weapon if he needed one.

He also had a good supply of lentils, rice, and dried peas and beans. He brought several cans of tobacco and paper to roll his cigarettes. To make his bread, he brought flour and baking powder and sesame seeds. He planned to walk to the ocean and spend a day now and then digging for mussels.

He also took along some clear plastic, intending to make a see-through roof for his house. But after a few days he found it was like living in a hothouse, so he covered that with tar paper. With some of the extra plastic, he made a kind of low, curved wigwam around some small limbs he had cut with his hatchet. The large galvanized wash tub went underneath this wigwam and the sun kept the water warm for bathing and washing out his clothes.

He did not take a clock, calendar, or a wristwatch. His timepiece was the sun. He did take a radio, which he used only until the batteries gave out.

"What kinds of books did you have on your shelf?" I asked.

"I had a complete set of Shakespeare," he said. "I memorized *Hamlet* and *Macbeth*."

"Why?"

"Because they weren't translated into French."

He named other books, though he could not remember them all—a poetry book by Dylan Thomas and *Childhood's End* by Arthur C. Clarke, some horror stories by H. P. Lovecraft, and some science books about insects. He took no art books, but had two books on astronomy. He had a three-inch reflector telescope so he could study the stars.

On the wall he had an enlarged map of Corsica, which had been his family's home before they moved to Algeria and then to Paris. When bugs or spiders crawled on the map, making a strange clicking noise, he did not kill them. He studied them, making notes in a small book about their habits.

"How about music?" I asked. "How did you exist without it?"

"I sang," he replied. "Sometimes I made up my own songs. I even wrote a little poetry. It was fairly good."

"What about women?" I asked then. "Didn't you miss them?"

At first he denied that; then he faced me. "I thought about finding a woman to come and live with me, but of course there wasn't room. Besides, I couldn't imagine finding one who wouldn't complain. She'd have wanted to go to town all the time and she'd have said, 'You never take me anywhere.'"

"You must have let yourself go," I said. "I'll bet you looked like a scruffy old prospector."

He was quick to respond to that. He did let his hair grow, but he shaved every other day and kept his mustache trimmed. He took with him four pairs of corduroy pants and a sleeveless vest that he had designed himself and gotten a woman in the building back in San Francisco to sew for him. He also had a Robin Hood hat with a feather. He had given all his other clothes to the Salvation Army, but had found in return two colored shirts, one maroon and one a very bright green to match the woods. He took along a bathroom mirror, so he could look at himself even if no one else did.

He had all kinds of small joys and excitements. He loved the sound of rain on his roof. On the days it rained, he stayed inside and read. When the sun came out, he tended his garden and watched each plant come up. He had never known how many small potatoes could grow from one plant. When a deer came and endangered his garden, he talked to her calmly, telling her that she had the whole forest to graze and asking her not to harm this small patch. The deer seemed to understand and went away.

He broke the monotony with trips to the ocean, where he watched the gulls and talked to the waves. He went into the grocery store when it was absolutely necessary to get flour or rice or tobacco, but he never lingered to talk with people. He did not buy a single magazine or newspaper.

"How long did you stick it out?" I asked.

"I'm not sure," he said. "I stayed until I'd used the place up. I stayed until I'd proved I could live by myself and survive. One day I just knew it was time to go back and I set out walking back to San Francisco."

"What about your books and your map and the furniture?"

"I left them," he said. "I'd used them up."

For Love of a Mountain

After the end of World War II we left Wichita, heading for California. But it was eight years before we got there. We had sold our house and furniture and bought a house trailer. The trailer was so loaded down with all our possessions that the clutch went out and we had a flat tire as we tried to make a hill entering Colorado Springs. We got the clutch fixed, but the rubber shortage was still on so all we could do was to patch up the tire enough to take short drives into the mountains without the trailer.

It was on a drive toward Cripple Creek that we stopped for a picnic lunch near a group of deserted buildings beside a clear mountain stream. A weatherbeaten sign read, ROSEMONT. Another sign read, FOR SALE OR LEASE.

The altitude and the mountain air must have made us a little crazy. When we returned to Colorado Springs we found the owner and signed a five-year lease for $900.

During the *Gold Rush* this place had been a town where stagecoaches stopped; later it was a railway station; now it was a place where tourists stopped to stretch their legs and picnic by the stream in the summer. There was furniture in the big lodge and in the nine smaller buildings that we planned to rent by the night or the week. We moved into the lodge and set to work, getting the cabins ready with paint and window glass. We watched fall give way to winter, and we were never ill—not even one cold. We blamed it on the altitude; no germs could multiply, we said.

Mt. Rosa was just across the road. It was the first thing I saw in the morning, when the sunrise made it sparkle or turned it pink if there was snow, and the last thing I saw at night, when the shadows were dense and full of mystery. It was never the same two mornings in a row. At times a cloud of fog might cut off the top as neatly as if a knife had sliced it. Other times the fog lay in soft pockets, floating among the rocks and pines. In September, when the frost came, a fringe of golden aspen began climbing up the side.

Each morning I walked across the dirt road to the spring, carrying two small buckets to get enough fresh drinking water for the day. I would push aside the green moss and make a cup of my hand to taste the cold sweetness. Walking back, I might stagger a little from the altitude. I would stop then, and look again to the mountain for strength before I went in through the back door of my kitchen and began the day's chores.

At night after the girls had gone to bed and Richard had banked the fire in the big pot-bellied stove, I would go out for a last look at the stars. They seemed close enough to touch. Then I would climb the stairs and crawl in beside Richard and feel the blessed relief of resting my aching legs.

But next morning I was the first up to meet the day all by myself. Before breakfast Richard headed for the barn, his knit cap pulled over his ears, his overshoes buckled around his ankles, and his windbreaker snug around his throat. He was a small man, but he looked stronger and braver than he had looked in the days when he worked in an office. He would come back from the barn with a pail of milk, his nose red and a smile on his face.

Animals, not people, were now the center of our thoughts and conversation. We had a cow with a new calf, a pony, a beautiful collie, a dozen hens, and one rooster named George.

Never before had weather played such an important role in our lives. For one whole week we were snowed in. The snow was so deep I gave up my morning walks to the spring and we melted snow for water. Richard had to dig a trench to the barn. George stayed in the hen house and looked bored. The hens laid fewer eggs. The girls and Rusty, the collie, played hide-and-seek through the many rooms of the lodge. No one interrupted "Ma Perkins" or "One Man's Family" on my radio. The mailman missed his once-a-week trip on Tuesday. We ran out of meat and had to eat a squirrel that Richard went out and shot.

Our only neighbors were Tom Merritt and Lizzie Price. Had they been in a small town, they would have been *living in sin*. At this altitude, nothing seemed to matter. We knew they were there at the big lake as caretakers and we could go to them in an emergency. They told us we were wasting our time and money trying to make a summer resort out of the old buildings. We refused to believe them.

As soon as the snows melted, the oil company came up and put in a gasoline tank so we could supply the tourists. We bought a gas stove with a griddle top so I could fry hamburgers quickly, but I was always afraid to light it for fear it would blow up. We fixed up a "dining room" with three small tables and a counter and stocked up on canned food and staples. Every morning, I made a cake to sell with the coffee. Every third morning I made lightbread while the fire was hot in my big kitchen range.

At last all the cabins were ready. Every bed had sheets and pillows; every window had curtains, if not blinds; every little private outhouse had toilet tissue. We put up our *Vacancy* sign. For the first few days no one was brave enough to spend the night.

I had read in a book that when Teddy Roosevelt came through on the train and stopped here, he proclaimed it "The Road Which Bankrupted the Language."

The tourists agreed with me that coming up the mountain on that narrow road was the most beautiful and exciting trip they had ever taken.

By early May, we were enjoying those few tourists and waiting to collect on our hard work. One morning, as I was making bread, I heard over the radio that Anne Baxter and John Hodiak were spending their honeymoon at the

Broadmoor Hotel in Colorado Springs. Just the week before, we had seen them in a movie together when we went to town for supplies.

Late that afternoon, I was serving cake and coffee to a couple of older tourists when a young man in jeans and a blue shirt, open at the neck, with no hat, stepped from an ordinary-looking Ford and called out, "Any coffee in there?"

"There sure is," I answered. "Fresh made." He was with a young blonde wearing a simple print dress, a little skimpy. As they came into the room and stood there smiling, I caught something familiar about her nose and mouth.

Then I screamed.

The older woman at the counter, who had been drinking coffee with her husband, got up from her stool and put her arm around my shoulders. "What is it?"

Richard heard the scream and dropped the gasoline nozzle. He had been *expecting* the gas stove to explode.

At last I managed to stammer, "Anne Baxter and John Hodiak . . ."

Everyone relaxed. The older woman's husband took an envelope from his pocket and handed it to John for an autograph.

The two stars seated themselves at the counter and both signed the man's envelope.

Richard ran back outside to pick up the gasoline nozzle.

I poured coffee for Anne and John with trembling hands.

"We tried to disguise ourselves," John explained. "We rented a Ford and wore these clothes." He smiled as his eyes went to Anne and her simple dress. "All day we've been going into shops at Victor and Cripple Creek and not one person recognized us. We thought we were getting away with it until we met you. I'd like to know how you knew who we were."

I explained that I had just seen them in a movie and that the radio had said they were in Colorado Springs. Then I went to get the girls. Karen ran upstairs to get a little autograph book she had in her dresser.

Anne hugged both girls. "We like to be appreciated," she said. "Just like anybody else. But after all, this is our honeymoon. We wanted to go off by ourselves."

"Every time we left the hotel we were followed by a mob of autograph hounds," John said.

I looked across the road at our cabins, all ready for people. "If you stayed up here, you wouldn't be bothered," I ventured.

Anne and John exchanged looks. She smiled and he said to me, "We might just take you up on that."

I pretended to believe them, but I felt sure it would never happen.

The next morning I was in the backyard hanging clothes on the line. A Ford stopped at the side of the house and I looked up to see them walking toward me. When they saw my shocked expression, they laughed.

"We brought steaks and wine and French bread and things for salad," John said. "Anne is going to cook our first dinner."

I took them to our best cabin—one big room with a wood stove in the corner, a dish cabinet, a bed, two chairs, and a table with an oilcloth cover. "My first kitchen," Anne said. "Where's the bathroom?"

I pointed out the back door to the privy, freshly cleaned and equipped with a roll of toilet paper.

John wrapped the meat and butter into a package and tied it with a rope to a tree just outside the cabin. "In the old country we always hung our meat from a tree to keep it cold and away from rats," he explained.

"John used to be very poor," Anne said to Karen. "I've always had everything money could buy." She looked around the cabin and took a deep breath of the cold air. "I'd like to stay here forever, but we've only got four days. Then we have to go back and make another picture."

We tried hard not to watch the honeymooners, but we were aware of them through every minute of the day. Two other couples had rented cabins, but they never knew who the other guests were. John borrowed our jeep and took Anne over the hills on roads that had been made for hauling logs.

On the third morning Anne came down to our café for a cup of coffee. I had just taken out my loaves of fresh bread, and the aroma filled the place.

"I've never tasted fresh-baked bread," she said sadly. "I always have to be on a diet."

I brought her a loaf, still unsliced, and set it before her with a plate of butter. After a while I returned: She had eaten nearly all of it. "I'm on my honeymoon," she explained, looking up at me.

On their last morning, the postman came in for his *high-altitude snack*, as he called the cheese sandwich, chocolate-applesauce cake, and cup of coffee he usually ate at the counter. As he was eating, I looked up to see Anne coming across the road from her cabin. I had promised not to tell anyone she was there, and I had kept my promise, but I whispered quickly to the postman and asked him to pretend that she was just like any other tourist.

Anne sat on the stool beside him and drank her coffee. They spoke briefly about the weather and then she returned to her cabin to pack.

As we watched her go I asked him, "Don't you think she's beautiful?"

He thought a minute. "She looks just like anybody else to me. She's OK, but I think *you're* better-looking."

The pictures Richard took of Anne and John that last morning turned out so well that we made postcards of them and sold them to tourists all that summer. One shows them sitting together on the steps of our cabin, looking happy.

When John tried to pay Richard extra money, more than the eight dollars a night we charged others, Richard refused to take it.

"If you ever come to Hollywood," John called out as they drove away, "you must come to visit us."

We did get to Hollywood, years later, but by then they were divorced. Later, we were saddened to hear that John had died. I followed Anne's life through her marriage to another man and the birth of her daughters, and I read her book about her years in Australia.

* * *

As the weather grew warmer down below, our business increased. Our cabins were filled every night and the cooking got to be too much for me. So I sent for Mama. She had been straining at the bit to come from Oklahoma and be with me. Before long she was famous for her pumpkin pies, made with real cream, her homemade bread, and her chocolate-applesauce cake. She brushed aside compliments by saying, "It's just the altitude."

Lenni became a guide to the beaver dams, charging five cents a trip and getting herself photographed with Rusty, our collie. It was an exciting summer for Karen, too. She collected enough tips to buy herself a $21.89 doll, which she named Patricia Betina.

After Labor Day, tourists continued to drive up on Sundays to enjoy the aspen, but none stayed overnight.

By the end of September, Mama returned to Oklahoma, taking Karen with her to attend school. She had missed a whole year.

We balanced our checkbook and found we had enough money to get us through to another summer if we were careful. Our days settled into a pleasant routine. With Karen gone, I left more of the housework to Richard. He took Lenni and Rusty for walks, gathered the daily firewood and, when the snows came, kept the nine cabins free of drifts. The outdoors agreed with him.

I took advantage of the quiet days to start writing again. I decided to get a new ribbon for my old pink portable typewriter, and set aside several hours every day for writing. By early spring, a few of my stories and articles had been accepted. I rejoiced each time I got a small check.

One day the postman was running too late to come in for his snack. As he drove away I flipped through my weekly mail until I found an airmail stamp on a letter to me with the return address from *Woman's Day*. The letter began: "I am glad to at last be able to offer you $400 for your story, *Texas Fever*."

I felt a wild urge to tell someone, but no one was near. I could hear the sound of Richard's ax in the woods above the house. Lenni was playing in the front yard with Rusty. I was alone with no one except my mountain. I ran across the road to look up at Mt. Rosa, waving my arms, shouting, "Thank you, thank you!"

A car pulled to a stop and two couples leaped from their seats and ran toward me. They seemed frightened, but as I ran toward them, I yelled, "I sold a story for $400!"

I couldn't have shared my joy with nicer people. Even the two men embraced me as if we were old friends.

Richard noticed the commotion and came running, the ax still in his hand. He was delighted with my news and he embraced me, too. Lenni and Rusty came running. They weren't impressed. We all had a root beer and nobody had to pay. We were rich!

As soon as the snow was gone, tourists began coming up the hill again and stopping. We kept the gasoline tank ready and the coffee hot. I still loved each day as I watched my mountain. I still got up at sunrise and carried water from the spring. Except now some of the newness had worn off. I knew we could not stay in our ghost town forever. Lenni would be ready for kindergarten in the fall.

That second summer at Rosemont I had even more to brag about to the tourists. They were to look for my story in *Woman's Day*.

Karen and Mama came as soon as school was over in Oklahoma. We had a busy summer, but we knew it was the end of our Rosemont adventure. When we totaled up our summer profits, we found we had only enough to rent a house in Victor, where I got a job teaching second grade and Richard found a bookkeeping job in a garage.

We sold the cow and chickens and gave Rusty to the couple who were the caretakers at the lake. We left most of the furniture there, since it had come with the place.

I promised myself and everyone who would listen that I would keep on with my writing, now that I had been published in a national magazine. But there is something about teaching that robs one of energy for creative activity. Now that I thought of myself as a teacher, a mother, a Girl Scout Leader, and a club woman, *writer* or *artist* didn't seem to fit.

I could see Pike's Peak from my window in Victor, where we lived in what was once a fine hotel in the Gold Rush Days. Now and then I got out my oil paints and tried to capture it. On Saturdays I taught a small class in painting. I called my art lessons *special lessons* because they were not in a school class. I taught just the way Miss Bess Bradley had taught me back in Oklahoma, not the way I had learned at the Art Institute. I painted enough pictures to hang on my own walls and I sold a few and gave away more, but I refrained from calling myself an artist.

In the Ashes

We lived in Victor for two years, then moved five miles away to the town of Cripple Creek. We moved into a big white house with a wide front porch and a lawn swing, eleven rooms, a back stairway, and a butler's bell beside a long table that could seat twenty guests.

Our new home had been built and furnished by a Cripple Creek gold millionaire who had committed suicide. It had been closed for many years until some distant heir had ordered it opened and sold. The satin bedcovers were still in place and only in need of airing. We could not pay the asking price of $5000, but they gave us a lease option for a monthly payment of fifty dollars.

We moved in joyously. Each of the girls had her own room. Karen had lots of space for her beloved doll house with all its tiny furniture and a corner for her favorite doll, Patricia Betina. Lenni had a whole bookshelf for her collection of comic books. She was not so motherly as Karen; she had tinker toys and building blocks and toy trucks.

Richard and I slept in the big master bedroom in front, which looked out on the distant Sangre de Christo mountains. In the early evening these mountains, whose name means "blood of Christ," were so red that I longed to paint them. But I had many other paintings that Richard had framed for me, the results of the two winters at Rosemont . . . views of the lake below our house, the cabins, snow heavy on the rooftops, distant hills with clouds hovering about the treetops.

We took down the old prints of grand ladies and handsome bearded men and Yellowstone Park, and substituted the pictures I had painted. Now I walked about my rooms and saw paintings with my signature on every wall.

The whole tempo of my life changed. I was a fifth-grade teacher in a tall brick school just a few blocks from our home. I walked there every morning with Karen and Lenni. Richard still worked as a bookkeeper in Victor. Our big house became a meeting place for Karen's Girl Scout troop and Lenni's Brownies. Our long table was just right for the monthly Methodist potluck and for the board meetings of the Culture Club.

The children played hide-and-seek in the vacant upstairs rooms on the third floor, or they frightened each other by coming up the back stairway. Saturday nights we often had couples over for bridge, with a raid on the refrigerator when we got hungry. We kept it stocked with baked ham and potato salad and beans. Richard and Karen shared in all the housework, so I had time for meetings with the PTA and for visits with the neighbors. I was in the center of a joyous whirl of entertaining.

With all this going on I was puzzled by the unfriendliness of a new couple who moved in next door, a house so near to us that if I'd opened a window I could have spoken across to them in an ordinary voice. The place had been boarded up for many years, and I was curious to know if it was as beautiful inside as ours. After they had been there a few days, I hurried home from school one afternoon to make a tuna casserole. I knocked at the door with my offering still hot, holding the two handles with kitchen pads. It was a long time before a tall woman with dark hair and a closed, rather pale face opened the door. She gave me a hurried thanks and then said nothing, waiting for me to leave. Later that same evening, Richard saw the man in the back yard and offered to help with the moving, but he was met with the same quick thanks and lack of friendliness.

With so many other people in our lives, we soon forgot our nearest neighbors and left them completely alone.

Three Saturdays later, after supper, we found ourselves alone and at loose ends. Richard tried to hold out for staying home with the radio, but I felt a strange restlessness. We decided to go to a movie. We walked the two blocks along the snow-lined streets to the narrow theater, the only place to go on a Saturday night except the Elks' Lodge or the corner drug store. Karen and Lenni ran ahead of us, holding hands to keep from slipping on the icy streets. We bought our tickets, laughed through Felix the Cat, and turned serious through the newsreel. We were half through the Patricia Neal feature when the manager came down and whispered something in Richard's ear. They hurried outside together. Then Richard returned. He whispered, "Come on, there's a big fire in the direction of our house!"

I had to pull the girls from their seats—they hated to leave in the most interesting part. When we came from the darkened theater into the night, the sky was red and flames were shooting up in the distance. As we ran home, stumbling across a vacant lot through the deep snow, we saw that the fire was in the house next to ours. A crowd had gathered in the street and men were carrying furniture out of our house. Already a few flames were eating along the eaves of our kitchen roof.

"The people who lived in the house where the fire started weren't home," a man's voice said. "They must have set the fire for the insurance and left town."

A woman ran to me and put her arms around me. "My husband went upstairs in your house and brought down all the pictures from your walls," she said.

Karen ran through the group of onlookers crying, "My Patricia Betina!"

A woman held her back. "You can't go in there!"

Lenni was crying now. "My comic books!"

Somebody laughed. I saw Richard go in the side door and return with my typewriter. Another man dragged out my file cabinet. All those things were from downstairs. I thought of the precious things upstairs and I tried to make a run for the door. Then I saw that the kitchen was all in flames. "My pressure cooker!" I cried out.

Another woman came to put her arms around me.

The fire engine was parked across the street with the hoses connected to the big hydrant, but no water was coming out. "It's frozen solid," a man behind me said. Across the street, people were gathering snow in buckets to throw on rooftops.

We watched our beautiful mansion burn. "Of course you have insurance," a man said.

"No, we haven't," Richard replied. "Not a cent."

A woman came up to me. "At least they saved your paintings," she said.

But where were they?

"Somebody must have carried them to a neighbor's house," Richard comforted me.

The third floor caved into the second floor. My mind recalled each article I knew was burning to ashes — my nine-star quilt that Grandma Clark had made for me . . . my wedding dress . . . Karen's baby book that had been there on my dresser . . .

Because our house was on the corner, they had been able to save the other houses. At last the crowd began to go away. We were invited to spend the rest of the night at a half-dozen places. We chose a family that had girls our girls knew. We borrowed night clothes and went to bed. I fell asleep, but woke up screaming. At first I thought it had all been a nightmare . . .

Next morning we rummaged through the things that had been saved and piled on a long table — a bag of clothing intended for the orphans' home, one tall black boot, a lamp, a box of my everyday dishes (not my wedding plates), my typewriter. At least I could write again if I ever had the heart for it. My paintings were not there.

A neighbor came walking across the yard. "I got all your pictures off the wall and stacked them by the door. I went back to see if I'd forgotten any. I thought somebody took them outside, but I'm afraid nobody did. They must have all burned up."

I looked at his distraught face and tried to comfort him. "That's all right, I'll paint others. Thank you for risking your life."

I looked down into the ashes. What had been so beautiful was now so ugly — a burnt-out hulk. My dreams of watching Karen come down the stairs in my wedding dress were abandoned. I could make out a bit of a picture frame and some kitchen pans . . . and my pressure cooker. One needs a lot of steam to cook at high altitude.

We moved into another house that had also been closed up for many years. The place had a mustiness that would not go away.

In the days that followed the fire we were deluged with gifts. Lenni's second-grade class gave her a comic-book shower. A high school girl brought Karen her own large doll. Eighteen women went together and bought me a pressure cooker, each one giving a dollar.

If I went to the grocery store or walked down the street, I was constantly met with the question, "Didn't they save any of your paintings?"

A woman who owned one of my paintings, a picture of Pike's Peak, put her arms around me and said, "I'll always treasure the picture you gave me."

I remembered those few paintings I'd given to others. I thought of the pictures I'd given to my aunts and cousins back in Oklahoma, and I said to myself, "The only ones I have left are the ones I gave away."

Teaching

"If ever *this* house catches fire," I tell Phillip, "be sure to save my blue metal trunk."

We take it down again and look at the jumble of old photographs, some saved after that fire in Cripple Creek, and some given to me by my mother.

Phillip is as interested as if these pictures told the history of his own family. He has lost *his* pictures. He once had a picture of his mother in a dance costume and another of his home in Algiers, the one that was left standing alone with rubble all around it after the bombs. But he left his pictures behind with some girl when he took off one morning very early. Now he longs to see them again.

"Tell me about this one," Phillip says, holding up a picture of my teaching days. I am surrounded by small boys. All of us are wearing cowboy hats and kerchiefs and all of us are smiling broadly. My hair hangs to my shoulders and I am slimmer by at least forty pounds.

"I was trying to look like Dale Evans," I say. "We were practicing for a skit to give at assembly."

"I wish I'd known you then," Phillip says.

I laugh, but I am flattered. "You were in your terrible twos about then. Those boys are all married or dead or in jail by now."

We go through many of the pictures, but Phillip keeps my Dale Evans picture out and props it against a bowl on the table. "I'll bet you were a good teacher," he says.

"I'm not sure," I say. "Maybe good for some children and not for others. A few times my principals said I was weak in discipline. One time I saw an evaluation of my work. There

97

was one word I'll never forget: *ineffective*. Such a terrible, stinging word. How could the man who wrote it judge? I'll always believe it was unfair."

"You want to hear unfair!"

Then Phillip told me about his brief encounter with teaching. It happened during his year at the Art Institute. Magdaline suggested that if he volunteered to teach art two mornings a week in a summer program for children, he would meet some parents who would be customers for his paintings.

He had no idea how to teach. He watched the children draw their little pictures with houses and stick parents and suns with rays sticking out, looking for signs of originality. He praised everyone's efforts. A little girl put her hand in his and whispered in his ear, "You're my favorite teacher."

Then his own imagination took over. He decided to make this class so interesting that the children would discover the same love of beauty he had learned from his own mother.

He wanted to include all the arts, so he brought in a group of musicians to entertain the children with the French songs he had heard as a child. One morning he brought a dancer who floated around the room with her veils. The children sketched her. He set up a screen and showed slides from the Art Institute. One slide showed Botticelli's Venus. A Dutch masterpiece showed little naked angels. There were statues of nude men with muscular arms. It had not occurred to Phillip to get approval from the school director.

His first sense of foreboding came when a father visited the class and said that his son's drawing had been displayed at the very bottom, in the corner.

"Isn't my child's drawing any good?" the man demanded. "Why did you try to hide it?"

"The placement of the work bears no relation to its quality," Phillip replied.

A week later, a woman in a severe suit with a wart on her chin met him outside the door of his classroom. "Our

children have told us what goes on in your class," she
began. "They say you show pictures of naked men and
women."

"I show slides of famous works of art," Phillip replied.
"Surely you don't object?"

"That may be all right in France," the woman said. "But
this is America."

Phillip felt that her reference to the country for which his
ancestors had fought was hitting below the belt. He rolled
up the papers on his desk and gave a shove to the table
where the projector stood, so that it went against the wall.
Then he turned and walked out, his teaching career at an
end.

"The world lost a good teacher," I said. I knew the
patience with which Phillip had taught me as he quoted
great books, played the classics, or showed me the beauty of
the Impressionists. I was often aware of how far my education had fallen short of his, though I have a master's degree
in education and he never graduated from any course.

* * *

For twenty-eight years of my life I was a teacher of children,
and only once did I fail to get a new contract.

We left Cripple Creek because, as Phillip often says, we
had "used up the place." There was no future in Richard's
job at the garage. Karen was ready for high school, and I
knew she should attend a bigger school with more advan-
tages. Fate may have had something to do with our decision
to move to California.

Though it was early May, we had a sudden snowstorm
that Sunday morning. We gave up going to church and
settled in with the paper. Richard took the sports section,
the girls had their usual argument over the funnies, and I
turned to the ads. A headline read: HUNDREDS OF
TEACHERS NEEDED IN CALIFORNIA. I saw the listing of a
teacher's agency that would get me a job for ten percent of

my first three months' salary. "Would you go with me to California if I could get a teaching job?" I asked my family.

I saw a flash of interest in Richard's face, but he answered as if I'd asked him to go get groceries at the store. "I wouldn't mind," he said.

"Can I go to a big high school?" Karen looked up with her eyes full of dreams.

"Can I start packing?" Lenni demanded.

I got my letter off to the agency that afternoon.

In a week I had offers from three schools. I chose the one nearest the ocean, a town called Greenfield. It was in the Salinas Valley — the "Salad Bowl of the Nation."

In June, Mama came from Oklahoma to go with us. She had lived in California and was anxious to return. She bought us a new station wagon and we rented a U-Haul trailer. By the end of July, we were established in a three-bedroom rented house. A garden had been left for us by the former renters. We got acquainted with our neighbors and spent a month taking short trips to the ocean and the California missions.

Richard started to work as a bookkeeper again in a neighboring town. Karen saw her big high school and could hardly wait for the first day of school.

At last I was told that Mr. Morris, the school superintendent, had returned from his vacation and would interview me. As I entered the school office, Mr. Morris stood up from behind his desk. He looked to be no more than thirty-five, with a neat, businesslike appearance. As soon as he learned that we were well settled, he said, "I saw by your application that you've taught in Oklahoma, and you've worked with the fifth grade. I think you are just the teacher we need for our overflow of fifth and sixth graders. We have a migrant population here. When the pickers move in, it disrupts the regular classes. Sometimes your room may have as few as sixteen, other times you may have more."

He was too polite. I was suddenly frightened. In my dreams I had pictured a room of second or third graders, loving and teachable. "I don't know . . ."

"I'll show you the room," he said.

We walked together to a rear entrance and went down some narrow steps. "We cleared this room of storage and put in desks. It's only temporary," he explained. "Next year you can have a new, modern room." There was only one blackboard and four rows of desks, too close together. The windows were half size. The bookshelves were made of bricks and rough boards.

There was a large geography book I'd never seen before and arithmetic books with fractions I knew I couldn't work without looking up the answers. The readers had stories I'd never read.

I worked hours writing out lesson plans.

The first day, I went early to sharpen pencils and put out writing paper. Then the doorway darkened and a well-dressed woman and a tall boy stood looking about the room. The woman came toward me with a fixed smile. "I expected my son to be in the regular sixth grade," she said. "It seems there's a rule here that if a child is new to the community, or if he's been gone more than two weeks, he has to go in the overflow room with the migrant children."

The boy was tugging at his mother's arm. "You go on home, Mom," he begged. "Don't worry, I'll be OK."

She did turn and walk away, but at the door she stopped and sighed. I wrote the boy's name on my pad — Thomas Page, Jr. He explained to me that they lived in the valley, but last spring his parents had taken him on a trip to England, three weeks before school was out.

Before I could learn any more about Thomas, the others began to come in. I took their names, thirty-eight in all. I set Thomas to passing out arithmetic books to those who claimed to be in the sixth grade. A fat, gentle little redhead with freckles kept standing by my desk. Her name was

Mary. She made me feel at home. There is always a little helper in every schoolroom.

I set Mary to passing out paper and pencils so the children could write about themselves — name, age, address, brothers and sisters.

Mary was collecting papers when I noticed a sudden hush. I looked up to see Mr. Morris standing in the doorway. There was no expression on his face except perhaps a touch of sternness. Then he was gone and the noise resumed.

By noon my hands were shaking and I had a throbbing pain in my temple. By three o'clock when the big yellow buses came into the yard, I felt drained and shaken. I walked about the room observing the destruction — papers dropped on the floor, lunch boxes forgotten, pencils chewed in half. If only I had been more aware of the time before the bell rang, I could have walked about the room with a grim face and demanded that they pick up.

My desk was a mass of uncorrected papers. I sat down to sort and grade them. Then Mr. Morris was at the door announcing a teachers' meeting. I listened and took notes along with the teachers of the regular rooms. We were to handle our own discipline as much as possible, because a teacher gets more *respect* that way. We were always to have lesson plans in the desk drawer and follow them as closely as possible, but their real purpose was to prompt substitute teachers if we were absent.

One teacher stopped me on the way out. "I feel sorry for you," she said. "Down there in that dark hole with so many children. But take heart. After a few weeks half of them will move on to pick cotton in Arizona."

Next day it seemed the room contained a mob whose sole purpose was to give me another headache. In my desperation I made rules: No getting out of seats without permission. No talking out. No feet in the aisles. I made my face severe and unyielding. I walked about the room, accomplishing nothing except a kind of tense quiet. I saw a boy carving his name on his desk and I hurried to the blackboard and wrote his name in yellow chalk. "Three marks and anyone who breaks the rules goes to the office," I said.

Billy was the first to go to the office. He wasn't really bad, he had just gotten three marks. He stayed a long time and when he returned he was crying. I had to get a paper towel and wet it to cool his face. The children were quiet, watching me, but there was no love.

I stayed late that afternoon, until I could slip unnoticed into the supply room and search for easy workbooks, crayons, modeling clay, and even primers. The papers I had graded revealed that in reality I was teaching third graders. Some couldn't read at all. I borrowed a hammer and nails and two smooth boards. I was determined to keep the bookshelves in the corner from slipping.

The next day I was terribly busy. A Mexican boy spent most of the day working on the shelves. Thomas made flash cards with the printing set. A small, dark girl who could not speak English began coloring in a primary workbook. Mary helped her say the words under the pictures.

It was three days before Mr. Morris revisited my room. He walked to my desk and stood there reading my plan book. He looked at the clock and then back at my book. "It says here you are having fifth-grade geography. You have books?"

One geography book was open. Jerry had asked me how to spell Fayetteville, but I didn't know and I had told him to find it in his geography. His grandmother lived there.

Mr. Morris walked about the room. As he left, he summoned me to his office at four o'clock.

"There have been a few complaints," he said at four o'clock, "about the noise of hammering in your room. You know how the noise carries."

I knew that. Lots of hammering went on all day as they built new classrooms, but mine was apparently the only noise that carried. I waited for advice on following the lesson plans. I heard a short lecture on how children

learned better in a quiet room. I vowed to take his sugges-
tion that I handle my own discipline. I would never send
another child to the office.

In a way, the lesson plans were useful. Thomas Page, Jr.,
used my book to learn what he was supposed to study. He
always did his assignments, keeping up with the regular
sixth grade. One day his mother came in to visit, just before
the end of class.

She sat quietly in the visitor's chair, watching me as I
helped Jerry write in his first-grade workbook.

As the three o'clock bell rang and the children hurried
out, I braced myself for the request she would surely make,
that her son be transferred to a regular room. Instead, she
smiled at me: "I don't know how you do it. How can you
keep them all working when they are at so many different
levels?"

"You must have been a teacher," I said, "or you wouldn't
notice that."

"I taught for ten years before I married Mr. Page."

"Your son is a very good teacher," I replied. Thomas was
erasing the blackboard without being told.

"I know," she answered. "He talks about you and his
classmates so much, Mr. Page complains that we have *you*
for supper every night."

When they were gone, I felt as if I'd been paid in full for
all the work I'd done. But Mrs. Page didn't leave it at that.
She went to the school board and told them how much she
admired the way I handled the class. And she complained
about the migrant children being segregated, as if they
weren't good enough to be in a regular room.

The president of the school board came to see my room
soon after that. He stayed for an hour, then asked me to
write a letter that he could read to the other members of
the board. My letter filled three typewritten pages. I told
about how it was in the crowded basement room with
children of all levels, segregated because they moved with
the crops.

A week later I was given my principal's evaluation to read and sign. It said I was an ineffective teacher and my discipline was poor. The other teachers all got new contracts.

We moved to another part of California, but I heard from one of the teachers in Salinas, who wrote that the next year all the children were placed in regular rooms.

Courage

Napoleon was only a name in the history books to me until
I knew Phillip. Now when I open a tin can I remember that
Napoleon introduced canned foods to the world for the
purpose of feeding his troops, and I wonder if he invented
the can opener. When I pick up a pencil, I recall that when
he found it hard to use ink out in the field, he instructed
someone to put lead in wood to make the pencil. His
armies opened Egypt to the outside world and discovered
the Rosetta Stone. He wrote the Napoleonic Code, a legal
system in use in the southern United States to this day.

Together, Phillip and I watched the film *Waterloo* on
television, and I can never forget how shaken I was at the
sight of all those men who died rather than surrender.
Phillip pointed out to me the actor who played his great-
great grandfather, who had been an advisor in the
Napoleonic wars.

At one point, Phillip almost died as needlessly as those
men who refused to surrender at Waterloo.

Shortly after he arrived in America, Phillip attended a
mid-western college that prided itself on its high academic
standards. It seemed to him that the students were mostly
rich and pampered. Many pretended to be Communists
because that was the fashionable way to rebel at that time,
but in reality many of them had jobs waiting in their
fathers' offices.

His first friend was a young German named Fraun, who
had seen his father hanged by his neighbors when he
returned from the war as an SS officer. Fraun was rescued

by the GIs and adopted into an American home as a displaced person.

Fraun was the picture of Hitler's human experiment with the "Master Race"—tall and blond, with steely blue eyes and a ramrod posture. He never believed in Hitler's methods, but he remembered clearly that every morning, the children in his school had to recite the slogan: "We are the end product of 10,000 years of evolution; to rule is our duty." He spoke with a thick German accent, but Phillip understood him well. Fraun knew fencing, which was the chief skill Phillip had learned in military school. At times their fencing got a little hostile, but never to the point of danger.

The French exchange students who might have become Phillip's friends regarded him and Fraun with suspicion. When the two of them walked into a student lounge together the place grew silent, like a bar scene in an old Grade B movie.

Phillip does not recall the exact spark that set off his disagreement with Fraun. He knows only that Napoleon had been insulted. Fraun took out his revolver and removed all but one bullet. He spun the cylinder and aimed it at his forehead. The gun clicked and he handed it to Phillip.

At that moment, a man at the next table saw that a serious game of Russian roulette was going on. He grabbed Phillip's arm and prevented him from pulling the trigger.

Phillip's anger was gone; all he felt was a sense of relief. He looked into Fraun's eyes and knew he felt the same way. Together they got to their feet and walked out, still friends.

When the news got around the campus, the two of them were famous. They were the *bad guys*.

* * *

Nothing in my experience could match Russian roulette, but I told him how it often took courage for me to face a classroom of noisy children if they got out of control. I said that getting married and having children could be frightening, too.

Phillip admitted he was a coward when it came to getting married and the thought of being father to a child filled him with apprehension. "But I did do a foolhardy thing when I went in search of Bigfoot," he admitted.

He had read in the newspapers how Bigfoot had picked up a huge steel tank and hurled it at a group of men working on a construction crew near Mt. Shasta. Phillip had just bought himself a new video camera and he felt that if he could just find Bigfoot and record him, there would be a fortune waiting for him when he brought the pictures back to San Francisco.

He was living in North Beach at the time, in a basement apartment with a large silver-tipped German shepherd named Baby Dog.

One day as they walked along a side street, another huge dog pulled away from his master and leaped at them. The man hurried to them and apologized for the dog's behavior. He introduced himself as Darrell Hanson and his dog as MacFrazer. The dog was part St. Bernard, part German shepherd, and weighed close to 200 pounds.

Darrell complained that life in the city was just too hard with a dog the size of MacFrazer, and said he was heading out to his home in Redding that very night.

Phillip had a sudden inspiration. Redding was not far from Mt. Shasta, where Bigfoot had been seen! He urged Darrell to wait until he hurried to his apartment, packed a suitcase, and got his sleeping bag and the food for Baby Dog.

Phillip convinced Darrell that they should track down Bigfoot and make their fortunes. Darrell said that he knew two men in Redding who had dogs and would probably want to go along. He laughed about Baby Dog's food, saying that once in the woods the other dogs would find their own food.

Phillip, Darrell, the two men from Redding, and the four dogs set out in search of Bigfoot. The expedition's first success was in tracking down two of the men from the construction crew who had encountered the creature. They couldn't describe it, but they showed Phillip and Darrell the ten-foot steel tank it had hurled at them. No way would they return to work, even at twenty dollars an hour.

On the first night in the woods, the two Redding dogs fearlessly chased off a bear. Nothing else happened, so the second night the expedition went higher up on the mountain on a narrow dirt road. It was so cold they built a fire and kept on their heavy coats and just sat on their sleeping bags instead of going to sleep.

Darrell was the first to smell the strange, repulsive odor. "Must be something dead around here," he said.

Then they all noticed the dogs. Even the two Redding dogs, who had chased away the bear the night before, just lay still, letting out low whimpering sounds. Phillip reached over to put his hand on Baby Dog. She was trembling in fear and her hair seemed to stand on end.

Phillip saw a dark shadowy something and heard a kind of growl that did not come from the dogs, who were still whimpering. He remembered his camera, ran to the car to get it, and started filming in the direction of the dark mass. (Later, when he was back in San Francisco and ran the film, there was nothing there.)

The thing left and not one of the four men got up from around the fire to chase it. The madness of the whole venture hit Phillip. He remembered the joke about the dog who chased a car. What would the dog do if he caught it?

Three pairs of eyes were looking at Phillip. It was as if the three men were asking him, "What kind of a mess did you get us into?" The romance of the adventure was gone. They sat shivering, waiting for dawn, the four dogs still with them.

The others ate breakfast while Phillip fed Baby Dog. He was too distraught to eat anything. They got into the car and headed back downhill.

Suddenly there was an explosion. A tire went out and the car rolled over the embankment and caught fire. Phillip grabbed his camera and got free. The three others braved the flames to get their duffle bags, but Phillip failed to get his. MacFrazer and the two Redding dogs ran howling into the woods, but Baby Dog stopped and lay on the ground, looking up at Phillip with worried eyes. The station wagon burned and caught some dry leaves on fire. They worked at trying to put out the fire, which was about to get out of control when a car with two forest rangers drove up. They were able to put it out with their extinguishers.

"We saw the smoke and guessed it was you guys," the ranger said. "Strange things always happen when people go looking for Bigfoot."

Darrell delayed the trip back to Redding by going into the woods and calling for MacFrazer. The Redding men shrugged their shoulders and said their dogs would find their own way home. But Phillip had heard their high-pitched howls as they left and he was afraid they had abandoned all faith in human beings.

Phillip stayed in Redding for several days, trying to comfort Darrell for the loss of his old clunker of a station wagon and his dog.

"We told everyone who would listen that we had seen Bigfoot, but he got away. We tried to describe him, but all we could say for sure was that he wasn't a bear and he wasn't a man. The only believers we found were a couple of men who smoked pot and babbled about aliens from outer space," Phillip said.

"But you weren't really discouraged," I said. "You went back to San Francisco and thought up some new adventures. Baby Dog probably had pups who looked just like MacFrazer."

He laughed at that. "You made a pretty good guess. Did I tell you Baby Dog saved my life more than once? She didn't like me to bring girls to my apartment, either. She was jealous."

"So many things happened to you. I'd think you would have run out of courage to try anything new," I said. "Where do you get your faith in yourself?"

"I was discouraged *once,* for about an hour. Then I remembered the time my father took me to the Louvre. Napoleon was responsible for about eighty percent of that huge place. He may have died alone on an island, but look what he left to the world. He changed it. I can't really fail, any more than he could. I grew up during the war, I'm not even supposed to be alive. I've been vaccinated with life, so I'll never catch real failure. I might see *change,* but I won't fail."

Making It Together

Why are Phillip and I still together? I know the needs that brought us together — my need for someone to share the daily loneliness, his need to have a secure place to call home. But I sometimes wonder if his feelings for me are merely territorial. I've noticed a look of jealousy if I speak too much of my life with Richard or Jess. And I've had strange pangs when he tells me the details of his life with the women he has known. I want him to stop thinking about them and think only of the joy of this moment.

"Do you think there is a kind of chemistry between us?" I ask. I am thinking of the closeness we share that is beyond sex . . . how we work together in the kitchen wordlessly, Phillip making the dishes he is good at — rice and macaroni and mashed potatoes; me seasoning the stew and making brown gravy; Phillip opening the wine bottle with his strong hands and then pouring the red wine into tall stemmed glasses . . . even for everyday; me placing the napkins and waiting for him to pull out my chair.

"Absolutely, we do have chemistry," he answers. "I'm not an easy person to live with. You'd have kicked me out long ago if we didn't have something between us."

I am silent, thinking of my fear that he may drop cigarette ashes on my carpet or forget to lock the door and turn out the lights when he comes in late at night. I also think of the other side of the coin — how he finds my glasses when I lay them down and stagger about trying to find them; how he helps me back the car in when I'm in a tight place; how he looks after my purse when I leave it behind some chair.

112

"Have you had this same chemistry with all the other women you've lived with?" I ask.

He is silent. "Sometimes, for a while, at least . . . did I ever tell you about Sandra?"

I shake my head. All those names of Phillip's women are firmly impressed in my mind, but Sandra is not one of them.

"I guess I just blocked her out," he admits. "That was a case of *no* chemistry. She came to my mind when you were telling me about your life in Colorado."

He had already told me about the free ride he had with a woman who advertised herself as a psychologist. He rode in the front seat with her all the way from Chicago to Denver. It was another time when being good company, being able to listen and ask intelligent questions, had paid for food and gasoline. When they got to Denver, this woman rented a large house and offered him a free room upstairs, but he declined. He could see the relief on her face. They had talked so much they had *used each other up.*

He found a cheap room on the other side of Denver. With his rent paid for a month, there was enough money left to eat for a few weeks if he was careful. Nearby was a restaurant where his kind of people hung out—offbeat intellectuals, unpublished writers, musicians awaiting a hit record, a few teachers, and one art student who took to sketching Phillip every time he ate there, the goatee and cravat making the subject so easy to identify that the artist could get a likeness in two minutes.

The best feature of the place was the back room. On certain days men met there to play chess for money. Phillip knew this about himself: He could play best if he was hungry. He had learned the game when he was seven from his older cousin, whom he could soon beat.

Forgetting that it was the day before Thanksgiving, he went to the restaurant expecting to eat well after the usual Wednesday afternoon game, only to find the back room empty.

With the last coins left in his pocket, he ordered a cup of coffee and a cheese sandwich. He sat for a long time, making the food last. Alone at another table he saw a girl, also drinking coffee. The first thing he noticed about her were her black boots. They were of fine leather and designs were carved around the tops. They must have cost a lot of money, he realized, remembering similar boots he had once worn. The rest of the girl was ordinary—black pants and a plaid flannel shirt. Her stringy black hair was tied with a black scarf.

When she got up to leave, he followed her outside and watched as she got into a red MG. He walked over and touched the hood.

"Not a bad-looking car," he said.

She pointed to the door. "You like it? Get in."

They headed north. Phillip started to explain that he lived in the opposite direction, but he kept his mouth shut. It had been weeks since he'd been in a car, let alone a red MG.

As the traffic thinned, Phillip savored every mile of the mountain scenery. It was as if he had a paint brush in his hand, washing in the gray sky and the deep purple of the distant mountains. At last they left the highway and went on a dirt road for about five miles. They stopped at a mobile home, set beside a stream, backed by tall spruce. It was almost dark as Phillip helped Sandra carry in her box of groceries. A few damp snowflakes hit his face, and he knew the weather was about to change.

The trailer was warm and luxurious. "My father bought this land and moved this coach out here," Sandra explained. "He put down a well and built a shed and put in a generator. I even have a washing machine and a bathroom. After my mother died, he married a woman young enough to be my sister. So he didn't really want me around."

There was no bed in the place, but Phillip noted the softly cushioned sofa, which he knew must make into a bed. He also saw the padded benches on each side of a pulled-down table. He hoped she would make that into a bed for him. He could stay there for the night before she returned him to the city and his chess games.

For supper Sandra made two sandwiches of pressed ham and instant coffee. Phillip left the table still hungry, but he figured since the next day was Thanksgiving she probably had a turkey thawing in the shed. He was already learning that she did not expect much out of life and that she spoke only when necessary. As he helped her make the couch into a bed, he saw her take a .357 Magnum from a drawer and slip it under her pillow. He waited for her to ask him to help fold up the table and make the two benches into another bed. But she got an extra pillow from the little closet and gave him a look that was an unmistakable invitation. She handed him a pair of her pajamas before she headed for the bathroom. He figured he could pretend to be ardent for one night.

When he awoke next morning, he heard pistol shots and looked through the small window to see Sandra boot-deep in snow, firing toward a small circle she had painted on a tree. Everything outside was white. He got out of bed and opened the door a crack. The car was now a big white lump. He was starving . . . and stranded.

When Sandra came inside, she shook the snow from her boots and changed into house slippers. "Breakfast?" she asked.

Phillip nodded. He was getting used to her one-word sentences. But his dream of bacon and eggs and toast faded quickly as she took two small packages of corn flakes from the cupboard. She slit them open so that they could eat directly from the box — with the instant milk she mixed from another package.

After breakfast he borrowed her tall boots and walked outside. He was fascinated by the silent, maybe too silent beauty. There were no log cabins snuggled against hillsides with smoke coming from the chimneys, no distant cattle huddled beside red barns, no fences to cast a shadow in the deep snow.

When Phillip returned to the trailer, he could hear the gentle thump of the washing machine. Sandra handed him one of her plaid shirts and a pair of black slacks. The shirt fit perfectly, and the pants did too if he rolled up the legs. He relaxed for a while on the couch until he became aware that the sun patterns on the floor had gone.

"Do you think we're going to be snowed in?" he asked.

"You might say that," Sandra replied. "Do you have any appointments for next Monday?"

He laughed, realizing this was about as near humor as he could expect from Sandra. "Do you expect any of the neighbors to drop in?"

"No neighbors," she replied.

"Are there any tame animals around?"

"I had a yellow tomcat once," Sandra replied. "One day he left and never came back."

The only feeling he could muster was a little sympathy for the cat. Being snowed in with Sandra was not quite like the dreams he had once had of being alone with some woman, no neighbors or animals for distraction, nothing to do but go to bed. "It's Thanksgiving," he said brightly, hunger in his insides and hope in his voice.

Sandra moved quickly to the refrigerator and removed two pot pies. Yes, he could see they were turkey. She reached for a box of instant potatoes from the cupboard and a loaf of white bread from the breadbox. Phillip had always considered white bread in the same category as cardboard. He hoped Sandra would not notice the disappointment in his face.

Next morning when he looked outside, the car was an even bigger lump of snow. "When does the mailman come?" Sandra had already been outside for her morning target practice.

"The mailman doesn't come out here," she said.

He was about to ask if she could read, but he looked over in the corner and saw a stack of magazines. He picked them up hopefully, only to see that they were last year's issues of *Seventeen*. "My aunt brought them to me last year," she explained.

He waited awhile, trying to dredge up an interesting topic of conversation. Some day, he thought, he would be able to make somebody laugh with a story of how he had been kidnapped and brought out here as a replacement for a yellow cat. He would say that if he had been in jail, at least he would have marked off the days. He searched the wall for a calendar.

"Do you have any games?" he asked, thinking with longing of his chess friends in the back room in Denver.

Sandra slipped her boots back on again and went to the shed. When she returned, she was carrying a game of Chinese checkers with purple marbles. After chess, it was tame, but at least it was a game. If she had cared about the game it would have helped, but she played with the same lack of interest with which she ate instant potatoes. He tried telling jokes, but if she laughed it was as if she had been coached.

Late in the afternoon of the fourth day, Phillip borrowed the boots again and trudged in the direction of the main road. In the distance he spotted a jeep, cutting its way through the snow. He ran toward it, waving both arms. It was like sighting a sail on the ocean. The jeep didn't stop. His ship had sailed on, out of sight, over the horizon.

He slowly retraced his steps and settled down for another game of Chinese checkers. At least it was warm and dry and it wasn't costing him any money. That night they ate the last of the bread and the remaining meat pie. The box of instant potatoes was already gone. Phillip began to wonder if she planned to kill him by starvation. Then she handed him the key to the shed.

He was amazed to find stacked cartons of canned food. The first one he opened was peach halves in heavy syrup.

There were two cartons of Franco-American spaghetti, a case of pork-and-beans, another of ravioli. There were four cartons of cigarettes — not his brand, but he could make the sacrifice.

All ceremony at meals was now abandoned. Sandra got out a stack of paper plates and stopped washing dishes. They used plastic forks. There was no need for knives; the margarine and bread were gone. They ate the peaches from the cans. No need for Sandra to wash the pan, because all the food she cooked was flavored with tomatoes. Phillip began to eat only when he could hold out no longer.

On each trip to the shed, Phillip was amazed by how much was stored there in addition to the food. Everything that Sandra's father had tried to interest her in — and that she had rejected — was there: an exercise bike, a loom, a fish tank, and an easel. There were several canvases with blotches of blue and green, but nothing painted that he could recognize, even as bad art. He could imagine Sandra as she grew tired of each hobby and carried it out there to rust and decay.

With no calendar to record the days, Phillip lost all count of time, but after three days of sunshine, he noticed that the snow was melting from the car roof. He got a broom and brushed away the snow and got hot water to wash off the windows. He found a shovel and cleared a roadway. He was suddenly full of energy and hope.

"Tomorrow I'll see if the car will start," Sandra told him.

It was slow going, but when the car stalled, Phillip got out and pushed. The highway was clear! Phillip shouted and waved at every car. The city, with its tall buildings, was the most beautiful sight he had ever beheld.

As they neared his apartment, he hoped the landlady had not thrown out his things. He saw his street and began to peel off Sandra's heavy black sweater.

"You can keep the sweater," she said. When she stopped the car and he got out, she handed him three twenty-dollar bills.

He tried to kiss her good-bye, but she gunned the car and sped off.

It was, he soon discovered, the twenty-first of January.

Weeks later, he saw Sandra again. She was parking her car outside "their" restaurant. He thought of asking her if the yellow cat had returned, but he didn't want to get that close to her. He said, "Hello, how are you?"

She answered, "Fine."

More Brief Encounters

Because of his experience with Sandra, Phillip shied away from being close to any woman for a long time. Through one of the chess players that he knew in Denver, he got started in the import business and returned to San Francisco. His friend knew about some home factories in Norway where handmade ski sweaters could be bought for fifteen dollars each. They sold well in college shops for eighty dollars, and Phillip was able to carry on the business in San Francisco for several months before the market was flooded.

He rented an apartment in the Sunset District, not far from the Golden Gate Bridge, where he often walked in the late afternoon to watch the sun set. For other entertainment he fell to girl watching from his big front window, though there were not many girls to see.

However, there was one who lived next door. If he was home around five o'clock each night, he could see her drive her small blue Chevy into the garage and hurry up the steps.

Phillip guessed that she was a secretary. He could picture her in his mind as she reached her room, kicked off her high heels, and threw her little pillbox hat on the bed. She always wore a suit, and had her long bob curled under so that she looked like Jackie Kennedy. He decided he would tease her about that if he ever talked to her. He had never known a secretary and he wondered what they thought about all day. He figured she must work in another part of the city or she wouldn't take her car out every day.

The car was what prompted him to action. He relied on buses or taxis, and he was getting restless for a trip along the ocean or into the nearby rolling hills.

He managed to be at the foot of his stairs one evening at five o'clock when she drove her car off the street and into her driveway. He motioned to her to remain in her car. He opened the garage door and then made a low bow. As she came out of the garage she thanked him and they exchanged first names. Her name was Connie.

He knew that, just as he had wondered about her, she had noticed him and been curious. "I couldn't tell whether you were a businessman or an artist or a writer," she said, "not from the way you were dressed."

Phillip laughed. He was wearing a satin shirt of his favorite color, maroon, with puffed sleeves. He also wore a black cravat and, as always, sported his Vandyke beard. "I'm just a lonely man with no car," he said. "If you plan to drive up the coast some Sunday I'd like to pay for the gasoline and buy you an oyster dinner."

He could read quiet admiration in Connie's eyes as she accepted the invitation. By mid-morning on Sunday they were headed north. The smell of sea air, the sight of a lone crane, the tall, fog-dimmed pine trees, gave Phillip such joy that he was silent . . . an unusual state for him.

"What is the mileage to this place where we eat the oyster stew?" she asked.

It was a false note, like a woman chattering in the middle of a movie. "I don't know how far it is," he answered. "I'll tell you when we get there."

"There's a road map in the glove compartment," she told him.

He took out the road map, but he couldn't figure the distance to Marshall, and looking at the map interrupted the scenery.

However, his spirits revived as they ate the stew and sat by the window of the tiny restaurant overlooking the oyster beds. As they relaxed and drank a second glass of white wine, they filled in the blank spaces about each other's lives. She liked animals, but none were allowed where she lived. Her parents lived in Hayward, with her ten-year-old brother; her grandma lived in Fresno. She had attended business college until she got this job in a law office. She was engaged once, but she broke it off.

Phillip was entirely truthful about himself, but he told only the good parts, not failing to mention that some day he could be a count if he wanted to, but that he wanted to stay in America and let his brother take the honors. He told her that he was in the import business, which did not take all his time, so he was free at almost any time she wanted an escort.

After lunch, Connie was very quiet, giving all her attention to the narrow road that took the deep curves along the ocean. He liked that in her. It gave him time to enjoy the sound of the surf. But after they turned off the coast and headed back to San Francisco through the Marin County hills, she kept getting nervous that they were on the wrong road, or that the threatening clouds would turn to rain. Even the joy of crossing the Golden Gate bridge was not what he had expected. They were held up in traffic so long that Connie got even more nervous. In trying to overcome her negative remarks, he wore out his own patience and was glad when he reached his apartment.

For the next few days he gave up girl watching and took the bus to other parts of the city to eat at interesting restaurants that he had once not had the money to enjoy.

Then, under his door, he found an invitation to Connie's birthday party on the following Saturday night. He decided to accept the invitation, and to find a gift for Connie that would make him the hit of the party.

He remembered a gift some man who admired his mother had given her when he was a child. It was a tiny monkey, a marmoset, with a long winding tail. He went to three pet stores before he found one, and it cost more than he could really afford; but he decided to go all out. He had such fun playing with it for hours in his room that he hated to give it up . . . which made him a little late for the party. But he was dressed for the dramatic entrance. He wore his maroon satin shirt with the puffed sleeves, his cravat, and one earring.

Phillip entered the room with the marmoset held high in the palm of his hand and the tail curled around his arm. There was a sudden silence, then excitement as the five or six girls in the room gathered around him. He was aware of three men in business suits and proper ties in the background. Connie accepted the monkey with squeals of delight. Phillip knew that, until his entrance, the party had been dull. He set about to make a difference.

Connie named the monkey *Marmie*. She invited Phillip over every evening, and together they enjoyed all its antics. Marmie was so quick that they were afraid to take her in the car with them, so they stayed home until the Sunday when Connie's mother invited them to Hayward for dinner. Grandma was coming up from Fresno for the purpose of meeting Phillip.

The idea of going to Hayward held no appeal for Phillip, but he looked forward to the ride. By now he was getting a little jealous of Marmie. Connie was giving the monkey all her attention. And at times, when he started to tell her some interesting story about his past, she would get a faraway look in her eyes.

Connie drove him around the city of Hayward before she took him to her home. They stopped at what she described as her favorite antique store and Phillip bought a cup and saucer as a gift for her mother.

Then Connie drove the blue car out into what he termed suburbia, the type of place he had always avoided. They stopped in front of a brown, single-story house surrounded by a freshly mowed lawn. As they entered the front room, Phillip was hardly prepared for the crowd. He bowed and kissed Connie's mother's hand as he gave her the gift. He also kissed the hand of the grandmother and Connie's very

pregnant older sister and a neighbor woman who had
happened to come in at the right moment. He shook
hands with the men and said, "Hi there!" to the ten-year-
old brother.

Later, as they sat down to dinner, he saw that the chicken
was cooked with wine and rice. He knew the meal was
planned with him in mind when the younger brother
demanded, "Where's the mashed potatoes?"

They were served red wine in stemmed glasses, but it was
chilled.

He and Connie finally pulled themselves away from the
family, but he didn't enjoy the drive home, even though it
was just at sunset. He was very quiet, thinking to himself,
"How am I going to get out of this?"

When they reached the two apartment houses set so close
together, Phillip got out to open the garage door. He
waited until Connie faced him, smiling an invitation for
him to follow her up the steps. The steps had never looked
so steep.

"Grandma wants us to drive down to Fresno next Sunday," Connie said.

Hayward was almost more than Phillip could take. "I'll let
you know," he managed. He hurried up his own flight of
steps.

The next week he moved, during the day, while Connie
was at work being a secretary. He had solved the question
that had been in his mind about what made secretaries tick.
He got an unlisted telephone number. He always wondered
what became of the marmoset, but he was not curious
enough to try to find out.

* * *

One summer day, when Phillip and I were having brunch at
Denny's, he told me about the next girl he went out with. As
we waited for our order, Phillip began people watching.
"See that couple in the third booth?" he said. "Would you
say they are married?"

A brown-clad waitress was setting their orders of hot-cakes and bacon before them. The woman's expression did not change, even as she took the first bite. The man's face was narrow and patient, as if he did not expect much of life. They paid no attention to the waitress.

It was a different story when the same waitress brought our orders, mine the $2.65 Senior Citizen's Special, hot-cakes with sausage, and Phillip's one egg, over-easy, with toast. As she poured Phillip's coffee, he thanked her as if she had bestowed a gift, so that she lifted her shoulders and her ponytail swayed. He dipped into the egg and pro-nounced it "Perfection."

My first taste of hotcake and sausage was pure delight. I never eat sausage at home; I know it isn't good for me. This concentration on the taste of food is a habit I've picked up from Phillip. Another habit I've picked up from him is chalking up points against marriage. My eyes went again to the couple in the third booth. They ate in silence, no change of expression.

"Would you believe that for several months I took a girl out for the sole purpose of watching her eat?" Phillip asked.

"I've learned to believe anything you tell me," I replied.

For the rest of that meal and all the way home, Phillip told me about Ann Marie. He saw her first as she sat alone at a small table in a café where espresso coffee and rich desserts were served. Though she was alone, she did not appear lonely. She ate slowly, savoring every bite, her manner as alive as if someone were sitting in the opposite chair. He watched as she took the last bite of her chocolate éclair and looked suddenly as forlorn as if she had lost her best friend. She remained at the little table, slowly drinking her coffee. She had pale hair and her face was gentle, though a little plump. She wore a pink dress with a kind of ruffle at the throat and a small, brimless hat.

When the waiter came to refill Phillip's coffee cup, he ordered another dessert—chocolate mousse—but he did not dip his spoon into it. He took it to the girl and explained that he had ordered it by mistake. "You will do me a favor if you take it off my hands," he explained. "I don't want to offend the cook by returning it."

At first she blushed and protested, then she sighed and took the first taste. From then on she appeared lost in the pure joy of eating. She motioned for Phillip to sit in the empty chair across from her. Being so near to her, he could hear a soft moaning sound as she ate. Phillip was so lost in watching her ecstasy that he forgot the rest of the world.

"I can't afford to come here often," she explained. "Today is special, my mother's birthday."

He smiled at her. He had never known a girl before who celebrated her mother's birthday alone. "My mother lives in Paris," he said. "I'll have to celebrate her birthday. I'll probably go to a French restaurant. Would you like to celebrate with me?"

When she smiled and nodded, he gave her the name of his favorite French restaurant, where he was good friends with the chef. He asked her to meet him there, since he didn't want it to seem like a date. He wanted to keep the relationship centered around food.

Sure enough, Ann Marie was at the restaurant when he arrived. He ordered the *coq au vin,* and soon saw that the taste of chicken in wine was a new and delightful taste to her. He could hardly eat for watching the expression on her face. Another time, he took her to a Moroccan place and they ate lamb and couscous with their fingers, enjoying the exotic atmosphere. They were given finger bowls and tiny towels to clean their hands. For contrast, they met at Tommy's Joynt on another night for buffalo stew and mashed potatoes.

Watching Ann Marie eat, and searching out unusual places to take her, became a kind of obsession with Phillip. For a time, the world narrowed until he almost forgot his friends. He found himself living in anticipation of the meals they would eat together.

He almost gave up talking about any subject except food. It was as if the world had been created for the purpose of delighting Ann Marie's taste buds.

He learned that she worked only part time, which was why she was available whenever he called.

The night he was invited up to her apartment for dinner, he learned something else about her. The refrigerator was almost empty. She confessed that she couldn't even scramble an egg. Phillip's opinion of her did an about-face. He phoned for pizza and a carton of beer.

When he left Ann Marie that night, he knew he would never call her again. For a time he lost interest in food, even French dishes. He went back to his old habit of eating only when he was hungry. He also went back to reading books and going to art shows.

*   *   *

The briefest relationship Phillip has told me about was the one he had with Little Lindy . . . not just Lindy, but *Little* Lindy. He never learned her last name.

It was in Denver, during one of the times when he was about to take off again for another place. It was also a time when he was grateful that back in France, in military school, he had learned to fence and had gained great strength in his arms and speed in his footwork.

That morning he had found a notice under his door saying his rent was past due. To avoid the problem of where to go next, he sat on a bench and read poetry for a while.

He was carrying his books past a high school just as classes let out. There was a fight going on between a tall black girl and a short red-haired one. It was a furious fight, with lots of hair pulling and kicking and punching. A male teacher ran out of the school and stopped the fight.

Phillip heard someone call out, "Hey, Little Lindy!" just as the short girl came his way. She bent down and picked up her school books, which had landed at Phillip's feet. Their eyes met and he said, "Good fight, Little Lindy—that teacher shouldn't have stopped you."

The two of them walked along together. She asked him what high school he attended. He told her he wasn't in school, that his books were poetry he had been reading in the park.

"I never knew anybody who read poetry if they didn't have to," she said.

As they walked along he began to feel very close to her. It was a time in his life when he had separated himself from everyone else he knew. He reached for her hand and she did not draw it away. They were still holding hands when they came upon a group of boys. They were all bigger than Phillip and they looked tough.

One of them sauntered toward them. He had black hair and a thick neck, and he wore a dirty brown shirt.

"God, it's Randy," Little Lindy whispered. "I hate him."

Randy came toward them and grabbed her arm. "Come with me," he said. "And you," he told Phillip, "you butt off!"

Phillip put his books carefully on the ground and straightened up with a punch to Randy's middle. He landed blow after blow until Randy fell to the sidewalk. Then Phillip calmly picked up his poetry book and took Little Lindy away.

They came to a hamburger place. Phillip reached into his pocket and brought out his last two quarters. Little Lindy understood his embarrassment and reached into her shoe to bring out a crumpled dollar bill. They had enough for a hamburger and a Coke each.

They walked on to a golf course where they sat on the grass and watched the golfers in the warm afternoon. As the sun set, he put his arm around her to keep her warm.

When the golfers had all gone, Phillip and Little Lindy sat on the steps to watch the rest of the daylight fade away.

"I could go call my Mom and tell her I'm staying all night with Emily," Little Lindy finally said.

He thought about his room where the rent had run out, and he knew he could never take her there. His future had never looked so bleak. He dreaded walking away down the road alone, but he knew he had to go. He took her to the corner of the golf course and then he walked in the other direction, very fast.

He had lost his poetry book somewhere.

Karma

When Richard died suddenly of a heart attack at fifty-three, I had this overwhelming urge to pay for still being alive.

He deserved to live as much, even more, than I did. He loved our five-room house with the flowers growing along the fence that he had planted and cared for. He had spent his last vacation painting the house and fence a gleaming white. He spent Saturday afternoons helping me clean house. Only a few months before, he had walked down the aisle at Karen's wedding. He would miss seeing Lenni graduate from high school. He would miss his grandchildren.

Combined with my grief I had a sense of freedom, of being my own person after being married for twenty-six years. I tried to explain this to Phillip.

"I know how you felt," he said. "You needed to experience karma. I spent a whole year paying God for letting me live when there was every chance that I would die."

"The two weeks I spent helping to care for the severely retarded at a summer camp was what I needed," I said. "When I got home I wrote it all down. I still have the notes in my files."

That first night as I climbed into the top bunk in the girls' lodge I wondered how it would feel to wake up next morning with twelve girls to look after. Some of these "girls" were thirty years old, but they needed as much care and supervision as my own children had at five.

At breakfast, everyone looked well-scrubbed except me. Poor eaters got all my attention, good eaters went unpraised. Susan shoveled the food in so fast I moved the platter of scrambled eggs to the other end of the long table. Jane dripped tears into her oatmeal.

Then everyone went, *en masse,* to the rest rooms. "Honey, you forgot to flush the toilet . . . put the cover back on the toothpaste. You must wait your turn . . . let Susan go first, she's dancing around."

The everlasting questions, "When do we go swimming?" "Is there a dance tonight?" "When does the mail come?"

I searched on my green paper for the day's agenda. But since I'd left my glasses back in my suitcase, I had to find a counselor to read it to me.

Nature study is first for my group. The director is at his outdoor table, calm, with his exhibits spread out and some crawling away. (Maybe I can sneak back to the john for a minute.) My big girls react to nature study in a variety of ways. Jane wants to pet the small snake, and JoAnn wants to pet the director. He is a tall young man in his third year of college. One thing we can count on: a short attention span. Nature study is over quickly, except for JoAnn, who wants a refresher course.

In the briefing before camp, we were told to put happiness first. Any teaching or training was to be incidental. Therefore, we laughed a lot, we hugged a lot, we shelled out compliments recklessly. We walked hand-in-hand with girls who could have managed alone. We constantly made great, joyous plans, but for no future past two weeks. "Oh boy, Thursday night is the talent show! Will you sing a song? What are you going to wear to the dance tonight?" It was a world filled with incongruities, and it was not cruel to laugh.

Tom, who was twenty-five years old and wore a red necktie, sat in front of the lodge, talking earnestly on a toy telephone. Jane found a dime-store ring on the path and explained that it was an engagement ring. Davy had a stick in his hand and was directing an imaginary orchestra as music came out over the loudspeaker. Robert could not speak a word, yet he could grunt out "Dinah" in perfect rhythm. Mike, who was known as a *skitzy*, could leap across the floor of the recreation room almost exactly like a kangaroo.

I have never been a good dance partner, not before or after, but at camp I was not afraid of stepping on someone's toes or appearing ridiculous. The Mexican Hat dance, the Bunny Hop, and the Hokey Pokey came second nature to me. I learned that music is not just nice-sounding noise; you have to *do* something about it, not just sit and listen politely. Music is for clapping hands or swaying or dancing.

I may have scored highest as a baseball umpire. I never learned the game as a child and I turned off big league games on television, so I made my own rules. I just kept calling balls until Judy made a home run . . . and usually ran in the wrong direction.

It would be hard to find anything as rigged as our Bingo games. Not all the campers could read the numbers or the letters, but they all won. They kept putting beans in squares and when one of the counselors showed a camper that he or she held a winning card, the event was celebrated with loud cheers and prizes wrapped in red tissue paper and tied with blue ribbon. It took me a while to learn how the gifts could be distributed so evenly, but then I saw that a system of signals was in progress. One counselor would lean down and say, "Look, you missed this square. Put a bean right here." Then he would shout, "Bingo!" In the resulting excitement the beans would slide around a bit, making it impossible to check.

Then came the final day, the parting.

Ronnie, who was brain-damaged, stubborn, and affectionate, headed for the john instead of the bus. Once inside, he washed his hands three times and came out unzipped.

Janet had been laying plans for three days to cry when

camp was over. She did, and in a soprano so high I expected landslides.

Elizabeth, the one most likely not to succeed in life, held on to my hand as if she were going into deep water.

All during the farewell, we counselors pushed reality away by saying through our tears, "See you next year!"

"Nex' year," they echoed over and over until it became a kind of chant.

We were at the clearing where the bus took off, tears in our eyes, when another bus pulled to a stop and out jumped a male counselor wearing a Scout uniform with many badges . . . then boys in uniform. "The next two weeks will be Boy Scouts, *normal* boys," I heard behind me.

The Boy Scouts looked strangely uninteresting . . . their faces too narrow, all so much alike. I did not feel drawn to them. None walked with a shaky, palsied gait. There was no aimless chattering. Not one tried to hold my hand.

* * *

Phillip was moved by my story. I was glad that when I returned home that August so many years ago I had written it all down in a notebook and saved it. That is my best/worst trait—saving everything.

Phillip, on the other hand, has thrown away everything he ever owned. But his mind records everything and he never forgets the smallest detail. For example, the year he spent as an unpaid volunteer at a soup kitchen. It was in San Francisco, in the early 1970s. He had survived the 1960s, he was making a good living with his video camera, and he was beginning to get a foothold in the advertising field. But he was suddenly taken with fierce headaches, which proved to be caused by an aneurysm on the brain. Given a ten percent chance to live through the operation, he made a deal with God. He promised a year of public service if his life was saved. God won. "You don't break a promise like that," Phillip said, but he added, "For no amount of pay would I have worked as hard as I did that year."

It meant sleeping on a hard bed in a monastery, getting up at six-thirty, going bleary-eyed to open the front door, stepping over sleeping men in the doorway, being the first to enter the vast kitchen with its huge tables and ovens and vats. He started the coffee and then looked over the produce brought in from stores — all a little damaged.

As other workers came in and found aprons, he first set them to making the salad — finding the lettuce heads, popping them to loosen the leaves, taking out the heart, and then chop, chop; mixing vinegar and oil and spices in gallon lots; cutting away the good parts of tomatoes and carrots and green peppers.

After that, there was a conference with the other workers to decide on the meat dish for the day — stew or meat loaf or chicken à la king. Then the potatoes, always potatoes, and gallons of canned corn or peas.

Then the arrival of the trucks, with drivers bringing cartons of day-old bread, crumbled cookies, even slightly stale doughnuts.

As eleven o'clock neared, Phillip would go to the front door. If the line was already around the end of the block, he would call out, "More vegetables in the stew!" There could be a riot if the food ran out too soon.

There were two lines. The shorter one was for couples, mothers with children, and people on crutches or in wheelchairs. These people were seated at tables with the food brought to them on big trays. Now and then some dude stepped forward, took hold of a woman's arm, and pretended to be her man. Some women took this calmly, but once Phillip saw a woman reach into her purse and stab a man in the stomach. The man staggered to the curb. No one got out of line to help. Finally an ambulance arrived.

He learned to measure the time of the month by the length of the line. After the first of the month many people bought groceries and ate at home for a while. But many people came even early in the month because they had no address to receive relief checks. Early November meant rain and people in the lines huddling closer together.

Knowing Thanksgiving would be the biggest day of the year, they started cooking turkeys at the rate of fifty a day, slicing off the meat to freeze, using the spare parts for stew. The turkeys came from various charities. School children saved their pennies and donated them. One boy brought a frozen turkey in a little red wagon.

One pet turkey came live in a cage. One of the cooks asked Phillip to put its head on the chopping block. The cook hacked away at it with his meat cleaver, but the turkey got away, spilling blood on the man's apron. A black woman, one of the volunteers, captured it and killed it with one chop.

The day before Thanksgiving, a woman came in with one pumpkin pie to donate. What do you do with one pumpkin pie? Phillip thanked her.

At eleven o'clock on the big day, the mayor was there, handing out the first tray of turkey and gravy, mashed potatoes, and dressing. There were flashbulbs going off and a television crew. There were also society women, aprons over their elegant suits, diamonds on their fingers, handing out trays. It was a day to be seen doing charity, a day when those in the lines turned their heads to avoid interviews.

Now, years later, as Phillip paced the floor of our living room, he tried to find answers to questions that had puzzled him at the time. Why were there never any Asians in the line, except for the Boat People, who were newly arrived? Why were the American Indians the most pitiful of all the homeless? Why did some people feel they had to complain, even when the food was free? "Hey, man, we had peas yesterday." Why were women often protective of their men even when they were being abused by them? Once

Phillip made the mistake of trying to help a black woman
when her man was hitting her in the face. When Phillip
grabbed the man's arm and tried to pull him away, the
woman turned on him and told him to mind his own
business.

Funny things did happen, even in that sad, hungry line.
One day a man, obviously a tourist, wearing white pants
and a short-sleeved shirt, pulled out his wallet to pay.

"Nobody pays here," Phillip said. "Put your wallet away
before somebody steals it."

"My God," the man said. "I saw this long line and
thought it must be the best place to eat in San Francisco."

Phillip had his favorite customers. One was a girl he
wanted to know better. He wanted to see what would happen if she were in a real restaurant, surrounded by ordinary people. He had Fridays off, so he met her at the bar in
a nearby restaurant. They had a drink and then, before
they got a table, they had to stand in line. It seemed so
funny to both of them that they laughed until people
stared. Next day, as she stood in the other line, she met his
eyes and said, "Thank you."

You need to live in the same house with Phillip, as I have,
to know that being head cook at a free kitchen was not for
him. Now he sleeps until nine o'clock every morning,
unless I tap on his door and tell him there is work to be
done.

I know he volunteered there because of the vow he'd
made. But I know the other reasons he worked there, too,
to pay for all the smaller sins that had gone unpunished in
his life . . . the time he hid in the closet of his room to
escape the girl he had fallen out of love with (the sorrow in
her face when she opened the closet door and saw him
crouching there, the way her shoulders sagged as she shut
it) . . . the money he had spent recklessly, that his mother
had meant for his education . . . the disappointment in his
father's face that last time he saw him . . . the way he had
taken off without even a handclasp or a hug.

When they see me with Phillip, some people are greatly puzzled. It shows in their faces. Some say, "He seems like such a nice young man."

Sometimes I answer, "Yes, but he's been around the block."

Some Survived

One of the things I often say about myself is that I am a survivor. That is because I am now eighty years old. My eyes are good enough to read as much as I want and to watch several hours of television every day. I can still hear perfectly and I have all my teeth, with just one filling. Both my mother and my grandmother lived to be ninety-two. I look at Phillip and tell him that if he doesn't clean up his act and stop smoking and leaving vegetables on his plate, I may outlive him.

"But I'm a survivor, too," Phillip says as he shrugs and throws out his arms. "I'm here."

On his fingers, he begins to list what he has survived. He was born by Caesarian. They thought he was dead and concentrated on saving his mother until someone saw his hand move. They rushed him and his mother home while houses all around them were being hit by bombs. The next day the hospital was leveled to the ground.

In America he survived being attacked several times by hoodlums; he survived a game of Russian roulette with a German who had insulted Napoleon; and he once jumped safely from a second-story window to escape a jealous husband.

He survived a brain aneurysm when the doctor who operated gave him only a ten-percent chance to live. He survived three automobile accidents. His X rays show so many broken bones that the nurses get excited when they see the pictures. He has steel in his legs, so if he tried to go on board a plane the bells would go crazy. He walked with a cane for three years.

"All that, so you could be here to help me up if I fall and lift heavy boxes for me," I say.

To him, it is not strange that he landed here in this small town to care for and be company for an older woman. I can see by his eyes that he truly believes his life was all planned for him with this one place and one day in mind. "If this hadn't happened and that hadn't happened, we wouldn't be here," he says.

I, too, have traveled a long way to get to this point. "I survived the Great Depression and the Cripple Creek fire, the birth of two children and two marriages and twenty-eight years of teaching. *You* even survived the sixties and the Haight-Ashbury—not everybody can say that," I tell him.

"That was a time that changed the world," Phillip agrees. "I was right in the middle of it. I took part, but I was an observer, too, because I was from another country."

He knew the good part of those days was over when one day he was in the back of a pickup truck, riding with other long-haired, scruffy characters. They neared a corner where a tall young man stood, signaling hopefully for a ride.

"We can't pick *him* up," one of the men in the truck said. "He's got *short* hair."

As their truck sped onward, Phillip realized that his companions were as locked into their beliefs and illusions as the people they rebelled against.

"You have to hear the music of those days to understand the sixties," Phillip said. He hurried to his room and found among the jumble of his tapes: "The Times They Are a Changin'," "White Rabbit," and "Blowin' in the Wind."

Phillip saw the songs of that period as primitive calls on a conch shell, gathering the tribes together.

If you come to San Francisco
Wear flowers in your hair

You're goin' to meet
Some gentle people there.

"In the beginning it was such a beautiful dream — a real spark," Phillip said. "The Flower Children wanted things on this earth to change and they did what they could. Maybe what they tried to do was too beautiful and innocent to have a chance."

He sang softly for me:

When the truth is found to be lies
And everything within you dies
You'd better find somebody to love.

He recalled one of the first sights he saw in the Haight-Ashbury during the sixties. It was late afternoon on Fillmore Street. That was an area crowded with gloomy characters, and most of them seemed to be looking for trouble. Phillip seldom went there without some kind of weapon, in case he ran into a situation he couldn't handle just with words.

As he stood near the corner waiting for a bus, he saw the crowd part and people begin to stare. Coming toward him was a beautiful girl, dressed in white, with long, flowing blond hair. She walked barefoot, with complete unconcern, reminding him of Botticelli's *Birth of Venus*.

Then he saw the reason she appeared so fearless. Four huge German shepherds without leashes walked beside her, two on each side, in formation.

This was during the time that Phillip rented a large old house and the only work he did was to play landlord. His motto was never turn anyone away, even if they have to sleep on the floor. Roger Stanford was a poet who had never been able to pay any rent, but Phillip took him in and pretended his poetry was payment enough. His poems were sad and none of the lines began with capital letters. The two of them spent a lot of time sitting in places where they served espresso.

They met their first Flower Child in the bright sunlight of Golden Gate Park. She was no more than fourteen, and she wore flowers in her hair. She had other flowers in her hand, which she offered to them. They tried to ignore her, but she just stood there smiling. "I think you are beautiful," she said as she turned away.

Later, it seemed that these girls were everywhere—and boys, too. They played flutes and mandolins and now and then there was a small harp. They turned their flowers into bracelets and necklaces and braided them into their hair. Love beads were big. So were earrings and tiny bells. Girls wore bells on the ends of their fingers so that they tinkled as they danced in the park or along the sidewalks.

It was not unusual to see young people dressed as if they lived in the Middle Ages or as American Indians.

After a while Roger stopped writing sad poetry and wrote of happiness and light.

Phillip does not recall seeing much alcohol, but there was grass and LSD and, because anything American Indian was big, some used peyote. So many people slept in sleeping bags in Golden Gate Park that the stores ran short of them. Others slept on floors in friendly places like Phillip's big house.

There was no shortage of food. Places serving soup and day-old bread and fruits were set up. If one person had food, they all ate. French-fries could be bought for a quarter a bag. Many of the kids had money from home; some were even rich.

Once Phillip saw twenty thousand young people gathered for a celebration in Golden Gate Park, all of them singing and dancing.

But soon he began to observe changes. He blames *Life* magazine and other national publications for spoiling what was meant to be beautiful. The Haight-Ashbury became an ugly street. It reminded him of the way Europe looked after the war—windows boarded up, people screaming in the night, dangerous people with hard faces. Instead of love, he saw burned-out looks of desperation in people's faces.

Most of the real Flower Children were gone by then, but there was one who remained. Her name was Jeanne. She still wore flowers in her hair and long, flowing dresses, and sandals without stockings. She had a place in an abandoned store, and there she played her guitar and gathered children around her as she sang them sweet songs that she made up as she went along. There were cradles and low tables and beds and an oil burner where she cooked soup. The babies she cared for were the children of the Flower Children.

Phillip took to stopping by to help her. The children knew him and would hang onto his legs and beg him to stay. He tried many times to talk Jeanne into having her songs recorded. He felt she could be famous. But she always gave the excuse that she was too busy and did not have the money. Jeanne was a survivor too.

*   *   *

After the excitement of the sixties was over, and Phillip had given up being a landlord and had lived alone above Bodega Bay, he returned to San Francisco and rented an apartment out near the ocean on the Great Highway. He went through a series of jobs that did not really interest him, and none of them lasted long. One, he told me with a sheepish grin, was making phone calls to sell vacuum cleaners. He felt a woman would get more attention than a man, so he called himself Vera and disguised his voice so that he fooled a number of customers — until he was found out and invited to quit.

He tried all the downtown art galleries, asking for work. Then he found a place that was no more than a hole-in-the-wall. It was owned by an old man with a limp and a shaky hand. "You can come at noon and stay out front while I take my afternoon nap," the old man told him.

To bind the bargain, he handed Phillip a twenty-dollar bill. He must have known hunger when he saw it.

The two of them walked together through the narrow gallery. Some of the paintings were what Phillip knew as *crazy* stuff, not very saleable. There were some primitive oils and poorly framed watercolors, and a few good prints with names that Phillip recognized.

They went into the back room, where unorganized stacks of drawings and unframed canvases spilled from shelves and leaned against the wall. There was a table and chair and a one-burner gas plate with a coffee pot. The old man pointed to a cot. "This is where I take my rest in the afternoon, but I'll be on call if you need me." Then he indicated the stacks of drawings and paintings. "Someday I'll get you to help me sort out this stuff and list it for insurance purposes in case the place burns down."

"Where did all these come from?" Phillip asked.

"For the last twenty years I've run a kind of art pawn shop," he admitted. "I can't turn away a hungry artist. Not many came back to pick up their stuff. Most of it is probably worthless. We'll just go through them and see if we find anything worth keeping."

On the third day of his new job, Phillip sold a framed print for a hundred dollars. The old man told him to keep it all. The money came none too soon. He was able to pay his rent and buy a few of his most pressing necessities — red wine and cigarettes and a package of cheese and macaroni.

Phillip began to feel as if he owned the gallery. He certainly fooled the tourists. He did such a good job of making the paintings look good that people often lingered until a crowd gathered. On one of those afternoons the old man opened the door of the back room and stood there, smiling and shaking his head. When the people had gone he told Phillip, "I don't know how I ever got along without you."

This good relationship might have gone on for years, except that one afternoon the old man failed to come out of the back room at closing time. Phillip opened the door to find him on the floor, his eyes barely open. "Don't call an ambulance," the man begged. "I don't want to go to a hospital and have all those tubes in me. Just let me die in peace."

Phillip sat down on the chair and held the old man's hand. Just before he died, the old man tried to reach for his billfold. "Find my son's card and call him," he said with what proved to be the last of his strength.

Phillip was lucky enough to reach the son, a man named Thomas, on his first try. He was in New York, but he asked Phillip to stay with the body until he arrived the next morning.

Phillip did as he was told, sitting all night in the cold little room, opening a can of pork and beans that he found on the shelf above the stove. He covered the old man's body with a worn blanket and passed some of the time looking through the piles of drawings and watercolors. He found a soft-lead pencil and did a few sketches from memory of the old man's face on the back of one of the pictures. He dreaded seeing Thomas. The voice on the phone had sounded very definite, as a Thomas should sound.

Thomas arrived and attended to the cremation details without any apparent signs of sorrow. Phillip opened the gallery and talked to customers as usual. When Thomas returned in the early afternoon, he asked Phillip to make a sign for the window for a half-price sale. "You can cut the pictures to even less than half price if you have anyone interested," he told Phillip. "I'll go out to the back room and see if anything there is worth saving."

Phillip cringed at the sounds of cupboard drawers being opened and canvases falling. He was sorry he hadn't gone through the stuff with the old man. At last Thomas came to the door and motioned to Phillip. "Close the place and look in the yellow pages for someone to come and haul this stuff away. I don't think I'll save anything. You can see if the Salvation Army truck will pick up the stove and cot."

After Thomas had left, Phillip went to the back room and picked up some of the drawings. The backs of some were good. He thought he might salvage a few and take them to his room to draw some designs and portraits of his own. Though he hadn't painted for years, he still felt the urge. He thought of the men and women who probably went hungry just so they could use their time to develop their talent. He decided not to call the junk man or the Salvation Army that night.

He picked up a few more of the drawings and suddenly recognized one of them. It must be a copy, he thought, for it was the work of a well-known impressionist. He found four others by the same artist and rolled them up under his arm as he closed the place and left for his room.

All the way home, he thought someone was following him. Once he even thought he felt a hand on his shoulder and turned around. No one was there. Could it be the old man was trying to tell him something?

The next day, he looked in the yellow pages and ordered everything that remained in the back room hauled away. A dealer came in and bought all the paintings in the gallery at a great sacrifice, but Thomas accepted the offer and said he was in a hurry to get back to New York. He gave Phillip $200 to tide him over until he could find another job.

The following day Phillip sat down at the table in his nearly barren room and looked again at the paintings he had recognized. He suspected that some hungry artist had copied them. On the other hand, it wasn't like the old man to lend money on a copy, so Phillip decided to show the paintings to a man who owned a gallery downtown.

Two days after he had taken the pictures in, he returned for the verdict. He tried to remain calm as he stood waiting in the office at the back of the big gallery.

"I'll give you $12,000," the man said. "No questions asked."

Phillip nodded, afraid to say anything at all. The man put the money in a brown bag, all in hundred-dollar bills.

Phillip carried it away as if it were a sandwich in a lunch bag. He passed a bank on his way home, but he knew there would be questions asked if he deposited the money, so he continued on and put the cash under his mattress.

For several days he stayed in his room, not wanting to leave the money unguarded. But he realized he wasn't having any fun. What use was money if it only made him lonely and worried?

So he shrugged off his fears and decided to do some of the things he had always thought he'd do if he had the money. He cashed one of the bills into a hundred ones and got on a bus, where he began tossing bills out the window at groups of people. It was great fun watching some scramble for the money and others ignore it.

He gave a hundred-dollar bill to a kid who asked for a quarter. He saw a bus coming and boarded it quickly, but not before he heard the boy yell, "Hey, man, look what I got!" A couple of the boys even ran after the bus, right out into the street.

One night he went to the laundromat to wash his dirty laundry. He always hoped he might meet a girl there, but that night he saw only couples, folding clothes and trying to keep their small children from playing in the dryers. While his clothes dried, Phillip helped out by interesting a small boy in a game of *Which Hand Has the Penny?* As he watched the boy's bright eyes and eager excitement, an idea was born. It would be lots of fun, he thought, to amuse children with real magic tricks.

Phillip decided to take a course in magic. He found a teacher and invested $500 of his money in equipment. In terms of fun and satisfaction, that might have been the best investment he ever made. He could scare waitresses half to death by pretending to put a cigarette out on the corner of the tablecloth. He could make a twenty-dollar bill disappear and pull a coin from a set of boxes. Best of all, he could amuse children. He got a few paying jobs to entertain at birthday parties. One little girl pointed to her brother and said, "Can you make him disappear?"

One day while shopping at a big market a few blocks from his apartment he saw a woman and her two small girls standing by the vegetable bins, putting carrots and tomatoes and a head of lettuce into cellophane bags. He was so enchanted that he forgot to buy the one tomato for his bacon-tomato sandwich. The woman had dark skin and was probably Spanish, but the two small girls had much lighter skin. All three had black, shoulder-length hair and brown eyes. He stood there enjoying them so long that the mother pulled the girls away from the vegetable stand and said, "I'm sorry for taking so much time, please excuse us."

It was Phillip's turn to apologize. "I was just standing here enjoying what a beautiful picture you made with your girls—there against the vegetables. It made me want to paint again, watercolors."

One of the girls came toward him, smiling. She looked down at his empty cart. "You *ought* to buy vegetables," she said. "They give you vitamins."

The mother pulled the girl away, but not before she had given Phillip a quick, slightly disapproving look.

He forgot the tomato completely and followed the three of them to the checkout counter, where he noticed that they had a ten-pound bag of potatoes. He watched them struggling with the bags of food and offered to help carry them to the car.

"We have no car," she said. "We live only three blocks."

He carried the potatoes and two loaded paper bags all the way up two flights of outer stairs and into a small but very neat room that served as both kitchen and dining room.

"Your father should help you with these heavy things," he said to one of the girls.

"We have no father," she said.

He saw a small toy truck. "You have a little brother?"

"He's in nursery school," the mother answered quickly.

Phillip had a sudden inspiration. He could see how poor this little family was and he was sure the mother would enjoy a night out. "Would you go to dinner with me tonight?" he asked.

Later, when he called for her, Dolores closed the door quickly behind her so that he did not catch a glimpse of the girls. But he promised himself that he would buy them gifts — one for the little boy, too.

After dinner at Fisherman's Wharf, they visited the little shops and bought gold lockets for the girls and a toy cable car for the boy. At the checkout counter of one shop, he noticed a large candy bar. "Do you like chocolate?"

She gave him a glowing smile and he bought the candy bar, but she did not bite into it. As they went out into the street, she slipped it into her purse.

They walked up the two flights of steps and the door was thrown open by one of the little girls. He saw behind her . . . many children, all with dark hair and Spanish features. "Yours?"

She nodded, not speaking, then said, "I have six children of my own, and a stepchild of my last husband."

"We didn't buy enough gifts," he said. "I'm sorry."

"They can share," she said. She took the chocolate bar from her purse and handed it to the tallest girl, who took a knife from the cabinet drawer and very carefully counted out seven thin slices of chocolate. She gave them out and each one said "Thank you."

He did not see them after that night. As he told me the story now, years later, he said, "The thing I remember best about that family was the way the girl cut the chocolate bar so carefully, so that each would have an equal share."

The next day he took the sack containing his money from under his mattress and counted out $5000. His jeans had no pockets, so he attached a small leather pouch to his belt and walked out into the glare of the morning sun until he reached the Haight-Ashbury district. He came to the place where he had last seen Jeanne, the girl who played her beautiful music to children in an empty storefront. He listened outside the door to hear if she was still there, playing her guitar and singing her sweet-toned, made-up songs. He heard nothing, but when he opened the door, she was there, looking exactly the same. She still wore her flowing white shawl, her hair was still laced with flowers. She was holding a small baby, but she was not singing. She looked up suddenly and saw him. At the same time a small boy also saw Phillip and ran to put his arms around his legs, clinging tightly.

"He thinks you are his father, come back for him," Jeanne said. "He can't remember what he looked like." She gave Phillip a hug. "I thought I might never see you again," she said. "You know, we are closing the place here."

"You can't close," Phillip said. He took the money from his leather pouch and handed it to her.

"Where? How — ?" She almost let the baby fall from her shoulder.

Phillip pulled himself free of the little boy, who still held his legs. "Just take it — don't ask any questions," he said.

Now, here in our living room, with the fire glowing and the television turned off, as Phillip finished his story I had tears in my eyes. "I don't suppose you ever saw her again," I said. "Do you think she still takes care of those babies?"

"I don't know about that," Phillip answered. "But there is more to my story about Jeanne. I've been saving it to tell you until just the right moment."

He left the room and returned, carrying his recorder and holding a tape in his hand. He adjusted the earphones to my head and plugged in the machine.

I heard a woman's voice, clear and sweet; she sang the words:

> I walked on broken glass today
> And it made me think of you
> I wondered where your restless ways
> Have taken you.

Phillip stopped the music and looked at me. "It is Jeanne, and she is talking about me," he said. "I heard it in the record store and I knew her voice." He played on.

> The last time that I saw you
> You were strung dangerously high . . .
>
> I hope that you have stumbled
> On a lighter path
> And found the peace
> That you were searching for
> At last . . .

"I can believe you," I said. "She really was singing it to you."

I looked at Phillip and knew that for now, at least, he had found that peace.

The Sound of Silence

When the ranch where Phillip and I were caretakers was sold, we had to take my dog, Molly, to be put to sleep. Our new rent agreement in Sonoma said "no pets." It helped a little to know that the lumps on Molly's fat little back meant that she did not have much longer to enjoy life anyway. But we missed her.

I was aware, too, that it might be time for Phillip to be traveling on. I had close neighbors now who would look in on me every morning to make certain I had survived the night. He was free to go out and find work and to make new friends. He was free to take off, as he had done so many times before. There were no ties, no signed papers, not even any promises. With whole days before me, I could concentrate more if he were not around.

Phillip is a very noisy person. He sings in the shower, gentle French songs that are probably naughty. He uses any approaching holiday to search among his jumbled tapes for proper music. Just after Thanksgiving comes an excuse for Christmas music.

I have come around now to watching sports on television with Phillip. Baseball is his favorite. The divan serves him as a front-row seat, where he cheers louder than if he had paid for a ticket. When he watches boxing, he prances and darts about the room. We suffer together with each knock-out. It is the same with game shows: He calls out the letters for "Wheel of Fortune" and answers the "Jeopardy" questions ahead of the contestants.

Life with Phillip is so intense that when he leaves the house I feel a silence settle around me that is just as intense.

151

I say to myself, "Now I can get some work done. I can have a little peace and quiet." My trouble is, the silence is too loud. I begin to lose my power of concentration. I listen for the sound of the door opening and closing.

When at last that sound comes, my heart races, then it *lays down its load*. I have known that feeling before, when one of my daughters returned from a late date, or one of my husbands came in late for supper. But now there is a difference.

I do not say, "Where in the world have you been?"

I do not say, "Why didn't you call?"

I have learned to celebrate the now. Phillip is here. The silence is over and we move into a frenzy of sharing. He may have met a new and interesting friend, or found a new-old book at the secondhand bookstore. Or he may have brought home a new tape. He begs me to rest from whatever chore I've been doing while he puts on my earphones so the music goes through my bones. If some beautiful note hits home, I may put out my hand, my eyes closed. He grasps my fingers so that I feel the strength of his hands.

When the music and the television no longer interest us, there is conversation. No subject is off-limits. My age has given me the right not to be shocked at anything. We watched the tape of *Oh Calcutta!* together, and he blushed more than I did.

We make lists and give comparisons.

"What is the most beautiful sight in your life?"

I answer, "The Grand Canyon at sunset."

He never had that experience, but he flew over it in a small plane. "Venice," he says. Forgetting my age, he looks at me with excitement in his eyes. "I'll take you there someday."

I think of the places I've been — Victoria, Canada, the Puget Sound in Washington, and the beach at Monterey, California. Not half the places he has been, but I wish I could see them again with Phillip.

He lists for me the places he has slept. Once he crawled into a laundromat dryer, but couldn't enjoy the warmth for fear someone might put in a quarter. He has slept in airports, on planes, in an Indian teepee, and in cemeteries. Though he drinks wine with his meals and now and then has a glass of vodka with grapefruit, I have never seen him intoxicated. But that was not always the case, he told me. What cured him was waking up one morning after he drank a great deal of Irish coffee and seeing beside him a woman who was known for making thousands of dollars every year or so from selling her babies.

That is a list I can't match. I've been a little bit in love with lots of men, but now I can't recall their names. I've read books, but their titles escape me. I've loved a lot of children to the point of wanting to adopt them. I've spent money for the wrong things and made turn-of-the-road decisions that were wrong. But who knows? If I hadn't sold my home at the wrong time, I would never have been at the place on that ranch where I met Phillip.

We look inward and try to explain ourselves to each other.

Phillip knows how to push the right buttons to make friends.

"Sometimes I go overboard and put out too much," he explains. "Then I have to back down and cross to the other side of the street or hide in a closet to keep away from someone. They don't understand that I've learned all about them I want to know. They can't see how I want to move on to someone else."

I let that hit home. It triggers a fear. "I know you've been loved by many women," I said. "I see that love, for you, is an experience to enjoy for a while and then get over. Why is that?"

"I don't know," he says. "All I know is I've been able to get over it."

"Is that true?"

"No," he admits. "Not entirely. But I think they all wanted too much of me."

"But you've told me that until you lived with me, you never really had a home."

He nods in agreement. "Sometimes I've found it a lot easier to find a woman for sex than to find one who wouldn't chatter all the way through a movie."

Not to chatter is one of the things I've learned from Phillip. There is such a difference between talking and chattering. Concentration is the key word. Was he born with the power to concentrate, or did he acquire it? "You even read a newspaper as if it were an assignment in social studies," I say. "Then you discard it there on the floor as if it were a woman."

Phillip bends down to pick up the paper from the floor. He knows that his habit of living on the floor irritates me, but he can't seem to stop throwing his things about. This is one of my problems. Should I mention that this habit makes our place *look as if a cyclone had struck*, as my mother used to say, or would it be only my home then and not Phillip's?

"This is the first home I've really ever known," he says, as he folds the paper.

In many of his stories he has mentioned being *with* some woman for months at a time. Once he even held down a regular job as a window dresser in a big department store in Chicago. During that time he said he lived with a young college student who was so beautiful all the college men were jealous of him. But he left her.

What have I got that she didn't have? Is it age, his beginning to grow old, too old for more adventures, or is it *me*?

All I know is that Phillip has taught me the true meaning of the word *share*.

It is Easter Sunday. I have closed my bedroom blind to keep out the afternoon sun while I try to nap. I have to rest for a while from the excitement of the church activities, from early Easter breakfast in the big church dining room, from watching the children search for eggs, from feeling the energy of the choir as they give out music on the biggest day of their year.

There is a gentle knock at my bedroom door and I tell Phillip to come in. I know he will be carrying his earphones and I will have to postpone my nap.

"Easter to me is *Resurrection*," he says, as he adjusts the earphones to my head. He pulls a chair up beside my bed and begins to play Handel's *Messiah*. It is a little too loud, but I do not ask him to turn it down. I listen as the notes swell. Pictures come to me of temples and church gardens and the tomb where Jesus lay until he rose from the dead.

I see only the beauty of the temples, their spires going up into the sky, not the poverty of the peasants who labored to build them. In the same way, I try to relax into the beauty that Phillip has brought into my life without mentioning the extra work he causes me. I push out of my mind the monthly bills; the fact that Phillip fails to empty the waste-baskets; that he doesn't empty his ashtrays and leaves his jacket on any old chair he finds.

At times like this, when music takes over in my being, I offer up a small message of thanks to Phillip's mother, there in her flat in Paris with her other children and grandchildren. I thank her for making her home a place of music and art. She instilled in him this great love of beauty. And now he shares it with me . . . now, so near to the close of my life.